GOD'S SPY

CHRIS PANOS

Bridge-Logos *Publishers*

North Brunswick, NJ

GOD'S SPY
by Chris Panos
First printing 1976 by Logos International
Reprinted 1998 by Bridge-Logos Publishers
Library of Congress Catalog Card Number: 76-55451
International Standard Book Number: 0-88270-214-9
Copyright © 1976 by Logos International

Published by:
Bridge-Logos *Publishers*
North Brunswick Corporate Center
1300 Airport Road, Suite E
North Brunswick, NJ 08902

To my beloved wife, Earnestine,
who has stood by me faithfully through thick and thin.

Who can find a virtuous woman? for her price is far above rubies.
The heart of her husband doth safely trust in her. . . . She will
always do him good. . . .

Proverbs 31:10-12

Acknowledgment

Earnestine and I together give our deepest appreciation to Mary W. Stephens, our beloved friend in Christ. She has earned this recognition by her faithful devotion and labor.

In writing this book, we have changed the names of some of the people and places to protect the individuals involved—especially those still living behind the iron and bamboo curtains. The events are absolutely as described.

CONTENTS

FOREWORD

What was it that drew a crowd of two hundred thousand to Mangalore, India's vast Nehru Cricket Grounds a short time ago? Was it Prime Minister Indira Gandhi's appearance there? No, her presence a week earlier had attracted one hundred thousand!

Was it a popular Indian movie idol?

No, indeed! It was a very simple message by Chris Panos, a young American businessman turned evangelist.

Chris is a man who has never attended theological school, but who has learned faith through many exciting and dangerous experiences smuggling Bibles behind the iron curtain, as recounted in this book.

He came to Mangalore expecting God to do for him what He did for Elijah in the Old Testament and Peter and Paul in the New! And do you know what happened? God did! That's why the crowds kept building to the two hundred thousand mark.

God may not want to give you that kind of ministry, but He does want to give you that kind of faith, and this miracle book can help you get it.

PAT BOONE

FOREWORD

God's Spy is Chris Panos' exciting account of how he, a hard-headed young businessman, learned through his experiences smuggling Bibles behind the iron curtain countries to expect great things from God. I suspect that, through this book, something wonderful is going to happen to your expectancy level. As you read it, remember that God can do the same things through you. The potential of the living Christ in you is unlimited.

BROTHER ANDREW

INTRODUCTION

Chris Panos is, by profession, a spy. Along with His more sophisticated secret agents (otherwise known as angels) God also employs a number of human operatives. But since He employs them in the service of His kingdom and not of earthly kingdoms, Chris Panos was astounded when, as God's spy, he got involved with all varieties of secret agents. Since he started working for God, his phone has been tapped (by the CIA) and his hotel rooms have been bugged (by the KGB). A beautiful raven-haired KGB agent once helped him smuggle contraband Bibles through Romanian customs—possibly unwittingly. Totally on purpose, a beautiful blonde agent laid wait for him in his room in Moscow's Metropole Hotel—only to flee in panic minutes after he entered. In India radical student groups have tried to incite riots in his meetings. Hindu saboteurs have disrupted his electrical systems, sometimes blacking out whole sections of a city in the process. Mobs have rushed and stoned the platforms where he's spoken. His life has been anything but boring.

Chris Panos says, "Now I know most people are going to say, 'well, boredom is only natural.' But that's the whole point of this book. Nobody has to be natural. Why be natural, when you can be supernatural? Why be bored, when you can live a life of constant adventure, whoever you are and wherever you live? And if it comes to that, why should people be sick, or poor, or heartbroken, when they don't have to be? We must write a book that will give them the answer to everything."

And here it is.

Mary W. Stephens
Houston, Texas

WHO IS CHRIS PANOS?
By Tina Panos

A new born babe was birthed. He was to be named Petro, after his grandfather, a Greek Orthodox Priest. He was born dead, with mucous in his lungs. However, God intervened and spoke to his mother, Catherine, in a vision: "Don't name him Petro but Christos, after Christ.

Then, the physician, Dr. Cook, reached down, took the dead baby in his hands, put a hose in the baby's mouth, and drew the mucous from its lungs. He turned the baby on its side and gave it a spank on the rear and life was infused into little Christos. He was alive! Chris went through the process of growing up into a young man and later married me, the one whom he says is love of his life. In his early years, he didn't just think about God, he knew about God—he had seen Him in a park when he was 9 years old. At that time, he served as an altar boy in the church. He was touched by God, maybe saved as a child, but he had no teaching of the Gospel to grow in the Lord.

Later, Chris was facing death because of an automobile crash in Houston, Texas. The ambulance had rushed him to Bellaire Hospital but he laid lifeless, not expected to live. However, the Lord Jesus Christ appeared to him and laid His hand on Chris. The Lord said, "Chris Panos, I have called you to preach My Word into all the world."

Chris Panos came out of that hospital a changed man. He joined the Church and began to read his bible. He would wake up and read the Word of God at 3:00 A.M. every day before going to work. He was a home builder at that time. He loved the Word and would spend hours studying it. Soon after, Chris felt God calling him into the ministry. He left his business to follow Jesus with such a love for the Word of God.

In the early 60's, he began to hear that it was impossible to reach the Iron and Bamboo Curtain countries. They were being denied the Word of God. Chris started to pray: "God send me." He asked the Lord to send him where no one wanted to go. God did. Thus, Chris traveled many times behind the Iron and Bamboo countries. His cargo was the Word of God, bibles. He experienced many supernatural feats of God. God has blinded custom guards as Chris smuggled bibles in the 60's. Because he dared believe, the Word of God was able. Today, we hear a lot about the 10/40 window. Chris has been working in these fields for 35 years. Dick Eastman said Chris was a pioneer before anyone called it the 10/40 window. Brother Andrew, known by many as God's Smuggler, said to Chris, "You are a pioneer like I am."

One of the first lessons Chris learned was to know how to bind principalities, powers of darkness, and wicked spirits in high places. Whichever country he goes to in the world, he binds the prince of that nation. While Chris and I were flying into some nation we had not been before, he would suddenly bind the prince of that nation. He would always seem to know when to do that.

Chris was a pioneer, working in the 10/40 window with the motto: "There are no closed doors to the Gospel." He was going into the 10/40 window nations when it was not popular. He was one of the men who paved the way—a pace setter, carving a new roadway into nations that were closed to the Gospel. He has worked in over 57 nations, binding the powers of darkness. He has held 35 or more mass crusades in India.

At one time, the Lord spoke to Chris and told him to hold a crusade on the Ganges river in Banaras (Varanasi), India— a stronghold of the Arva Samaji group. Many Indian Christians warned Chris not to go. A Christian leader, Philip Abraham wrote to say that many Christians had been killed in Varanasi. Chris replied that God, by the Holy Spirit, had commanded him to go. Abraham wrote back, saying that if Chris came to Varanasi, he had to come prepared to die. Chris went and it was one of the best crusades he has ever had. The power of the devil was broken in that city. Today, there are a number of Christian works in Varanasi. This crusade prepared the way for others to preach and hold crusades. The vice chairman of the medical college came to Chris after seeing the demon-possessed healed instantly by the power of the Holy Spirit. He wanted Chris to teach the medical students how to have faith to heal the sick.

In every crusade, the news media would come to interview Chris Panos. He would never compromise in any way. They said they would accept Jesus Christ as another God and put Him on a shelf. However, Chris insisted the only way to the Father and heaven was through Jesus Christ. He invited them to the platform to see with their own eyes the miracles of God. The next morning, the newspaper headlines would reveal many miracles that this Jesus Christ was doing and the media could not deny them.

Chris Panos was instrumental in starting the Charismatic movement in Mangalore (200,000 people in one crusade) and Bangalore, with 50,000 Roman Catholics attending. The Lord gave him great favor with the Archbishop Arokisaswamy of Bangalore who was attending the crusade. He thanked Chris Panos for coming to India and said: "Everyone could sense that you are fully committed to Christ, and like the Apostle Paul, you are eager to preach Christ and Him crucified. I am extremely happy about the miracle life crusade you conducted here in Bangalore. You made it plain from the beginning that the Holy Spirit alone did these miracles."

Many sisters from the St. Agnes Catholic convent considered themselves blessed to have heard Chris and witnessed his work in teaching others to praise the name of Jesus. They said, "the crusade has given us added courage, deepened our faith, and given us a deep desire to call on the Name of Jesus openly. May God bless and reward your untiring zeal and labor to preach Jesus' life-giving words by open proclamation. It reminded us of Paul of Tarsus and his work. You are the second Apostle Paul, chosen by God to proclaim His name around the world before the glorious second coming of Jesus and the end of the world." "Brother Panos," said one of the sisters, "you may never know where your influence has started and where it will end in India and the world. We would like you to conduct more crusades in our country. India needs more apostles like you to preach the name of Jesus openly."

Just a few weeks before the Tiananmen Square Massacre, Chris was giving out hundreds of Gospels in the very spot where many had been killed. Pat Robertson said to him: "I wanted to thank you personally for the role you played as a catalyst to help establish a Christian radio outreach to beam throughout the Middle East from Cyprus. Your role in introducing me to President Makarios was invaluable."

I could go on and on with pages of testimonies of nationals whom Chris trained. I could give pages and pages of testimonies of proven miracles. Jack Reed, T.L. Osborn's nephew, was with Chris in Marthandam, India, and said, " I have never seen so many blind healed at one service in my life." The deaf, the cancer-stricken, and the crippled (some of whom had not walked for years and years) were healed. Those crippled from birth left the crusade walking.

In Mysore City, India, one leper was healed by the power of the Word of God. While Chris was preaching, the Hindus and Muslims started throwing rocks at the platform. They stormed the platform and started throwing those seated there off the platform. They grabbed Chris' interpreter's microphone, but Chris grabbed it back and told the interpreter to hold on to it. Our son, Danny, warned his dad to watch out. "They are coming up the ramp on your side," he shouted. Chris said, "I felt like a lion. I saw them coming and I started running towards them down the platform. They saw me coming and they jumped over the rail. Then, the miracle happened. At the bottom of the ramp was a leper who had had his toes eaten by leprosy. The man was healed instantly! He jumped up and ran up the ramp declaring, "Jesus healed me!"

One Hindu woman came to the crusade in Hubli, India. While she sat on the ground listening to Chris preach the Gospel, she saw the most beautiful man she had ever seen, dressed in white, standing behind Chris Panos. The man had the most beautiful eyes, filled with love. She immediately accepted Jesus Christ as her Savior.

As Chris' wife for 43 years, I have stood in the background and viewed many amazing things. Today, I hear of all the wonders that God is doing in the world. Now, I am convinced that Chris has been planting the seeds and others have been reaping. I know all this because God is not unjust to forget his servant's works and "your labor of love which you have made known in His Name, for you have ministered to the saints and still do minister." (Hebrews 6:10)

We appreciate all your love gifts that have made it possible to reach the lost in many nations all over the world. Doors are open in Central and South America, Africa, India, Russia, and the Far East for crusades and missionary work. It is by your sacrificial giving that fuels this chariot of evangelism. Please pray and stand with us in this hour of need and give the best gift possible.

Chapter One
The Three-Way Spy Ring

I was aboard a jet from Vienna to Bucharest. Our plane had hit rough weather; it bumped and pitched as we flew towards Romania. It felt somewhat like riding in a roller coaster.

"Please keep your seat belts fastened," the intercom requested. "We have hit some turbulence. Dinner will be delayed."

I looked around at my fellow passengers. Many of them were uneasy, and some were also airsick. The man to my right, a distinguished-looking Englishman, appeared very uncomfortable. Beads of sweat were standing on his forehead, and his face was pale. I expected him to be sick any minute.

Quietly I prayed, commanding the plane to be loosed from the turbulence and binding the prince of the air. Immediately, the plane stopped pitching and there was a sudden calm. Soon the smell of cooking permeated the air, and stewardesses began the disciplined hustle and bustle of serving dinner.

The man to my right looked much more comfortable. As we waited for the stewardesses to bring us our steaks, he turned to me and said, "My name is Alec Porter. I'm a salesman with UniRoyal. Who are you and what do you do?"

Porter had the looks and accent of an upper-class Englishman, but well-bred Englishmen don't make a habit of addressing strangers, much less interrogating them. I decided to be as unorthodox as he was.

"My name is Chris Panos and I smuggle Bibles into Communist countries," I said.

A spectacular array of emotions flickered across my neighbor's face. He looked distressed, annoyed, frightened and, underneath it all, strangely satisfied.

"My dear chap," said Porter, "please be careful. There has been a robbery of some very famous art pieces. Everyone going through customs is being much more thoroughly checked than usual."

"Don't worry about me. I'll be all right."

"Tell me one thing," he asked. "What is it I sense about you? There seems to be some sort of strange vibration in the air around you."

"That's God's power," I said. "My God has supernatural power, and He has given me the authority to use it."

"I am an agnostic," Porter told me. "I cannot say there is no God, but on the other hand, I cannot say there is one. But I must warn you again that if you are going to smuggle Bibles through the customs today, it will be very dangerous. I am a frequent traveler, and even I will be scrutinized thoroughly. Bibles bring a good price on the black market here; the penalties are very severe if you're caught. Please be very careful."

As Alec Porter and I continued to talk, the subject returned to the "power" he had felt around me.

"About this power you have," he continued, "where did you get it?"

"It's not mine, it's God's. This is how I get through customs; not by being clever or sneaky, but by the power of God. If God led me to do it, I could wear a sign saying, 'I am a Bible smuggler,' and because of God's power, I would still get through customs without any trouble. I have gone through Communist customs many times, and God has always taken care of me. He'll take care of me again today. You watch."

Porter roared with laughter. "I wonder what I've gotten myself into now? This must be what a novel is like. I feel like a character in a book."

As we talked some more, the plane began its descent into the Bucharest airport.

Our landing was perfect, but as we touched ground I noticed Porter was perspiring again. He looked very nervous.

"Don't worry about me," I told him. "God will protect me."

He shook his head in disbelief. "Are the Bibles on your person or in your luggage?" he asked.

"Both places." He shook his head again as we got off the aircraft.

When we arrived at customs, we found that every bag and suitcase was being checked and doublechecked, just as Porter had warned me. Because of all the extra security, the line moved slowly. Finally, Porter's turn arrived.

"Hello, Mr. Porter," the customs agent said, smiling at him apologetically. Apologetic or not, it was the first time I had ever seen a Romanian customs agent smile. "Today we must check your bags also. I am very sorry." The agent

3

checked Porter's bag just as thoroughly as he had checked everybody else's. Then he turned to me.

"Are you with Mr. Porter?" he asked.

"Yes."

"Move on through," he said. He marked my bags with a piece of chalk, and waved me on.

Porter was incredulous. "I can't believe it," he told me. "I simply can't believe it. Look around you. Every bag is being checked! Why, even mine was checked, and these customs agents know me well. Every bag was checked, Mr. Panos, but yours. I am beginning to think that perhaps this God you serve might exist after all."

Porter and I walked together towards the lobby of the terminal. There he was met by a friend of his, a lovely dark-haired woman who promptly gave him a big wink and then just as promptly hugged him. From the hug, I deduced that Porter and this woman were on very friendly terms. Too friendly.

"I am so glad to see you," Porter's friend told him. "It has been a long time." She grabbed him and smothered him with kisses. Next she wheeled around to me. "Who is your friend?" she asked Porter. He didn't have time to answer before she said. "Dahlink, I think he's cute!"

"This is my friend Chris Panos," Mr. Porter finally managed to tell her. "Chris, meet Madame Rozinko."

"I am glad to meet you, Mr. Panos." She looked into my eyes as though we had known each other well.

"Chris, where are you staying?" Porter asked in the temporary lull.

"At the Lido."

"What a coincidence!" he exclaimed. "So am I. Why don't you ride with us?"

"Yes, dahlink, come and ride with us," Madame Rozinko chimed in.

I was delighted to accept. My funds were low, and a few free rides would come in handy.

Madame Rozinko's car turned out to be a black Mercedes, complete with driver. She sat in front, and Porter and I climbed in the back. She and Porter kept up a constant stream of chatter all the way to the hotel. When we arrived we got out and went to the front desk. I knew the clerk, Mrs. Pappas, from a previous visit. She, too, was of Greek extraction.

"*Tikanis*," she said, greeting me in Greek.

"*Kala*," I responded. Still speaking Greek, I asked her to give me a nice but very reasonable room.

"There is no room," she told me. "We don't have one available."

"You have to have one. The airlines made a reservation."

"We did not receive it," she said. "But don't worry. We'll work it out."

"Mr. Porter," she said in English, "I see you know my friend, Mr. Panos. Something has gone wrong with his reservation, and we have no room to give him. But there are two beds in your single room. Would you be willing to have him stay with you? There would be no extra charge, of course."

"All right," Porter said. "Put him in with me."

I said a quick prayer of thanks. God had taken the airline's mistake and turned it into a blessing.

The Lido is an old hotel, clean and luxurious by Communist standards. As soon as we entered our room, Porter turned on the radio. The music was much too loud for comfort. Then he crossed the room and stood by my side. "Speak very softly," Porter murmured in my ear. "All the rooms in this hotel are bugged." I could hardly believe it. On the airplane, Porter had felt as though he were in a novel. Now it was my turn. I felt as though I was in a spy story.

"Make yourself at home," Porter murmured as soon as we'd unpacked. "I must meet with the Romanian woman now, but how about meeting me at eight for dinner?"

"That will be fine."

That evening we dined together on a balcony overlooking a beautiful courtyard. During the afternoon, Mrs. Pappas had told me that she had lined up some people who needed Romanian Bibles. I rejoiced. It had been a productive day, and now Porter was treating me to a delicious dinner. Once again, God was providing for my material needs.

"You look very happy," Porter told me. "I suppose you ought to be. I still can't believe what I saw at customs today. What is the source of your power? Just what is the key that unlocks the door?"

"The key is Jesus of Nazareth. He died and rose again. Today He holds the place of all power in the universe. But most men are not interested in His power because they're busy trying to exert their own.

"But, if you want access to His power you must be born again. You'll know you've been born again when you begin to call on Jesus to spare you and give you His life—eternal life."

"I know you are right," he said. He looked close to tears. "Please pray for me." Before I could offer to pray the sinners' prayer with him, he looked at his watch and said, "I must meet with Madame Rozinko again tonight. Please excuse me. I will see you later."

In the days that followed, neither of us mentioned the conversation we'd had over dinner. We breakfasted together nearly every morning, but avoided the topic of religion. He went about his business and I went about mine, which was distributing the Romanian gospels and New Testaments to the people lined up by Mrs. Pappas. Soon, I knew it was time to move on. That evening, Mr. Porter asked, "When are you leaving?"

"Tomorrow morning."

"I will be leaving then, too. I will give you a lift to the airport. Did you dispose of those Bibles?"

"All of the Romanian Bibles are gone, but I still have the Russian ones, of course."

Mr. Porter's face turned red. "You start praying now and really talk to God, because Madame Rozinko says she is not sure what to expect at customs. The guards have redoubled their efforts. The lines are very long. Security is even tighter than it was before. Pray hard and be very, very careful. And let me tell you this in strict confidence. Madame Rozinko is a spy. She is a member of the KGB and she knows what's going on."

Suddenly I knew, without his having to tell me, that Porter too was a spy. Part of his job must have involved extracting information from Madame Rozinko. I had considered myself to be a spy for God all along, but I was mildly surprised to find God's spy getting mixed up with the world's.

The following morning, Madame Rozinko picked us up to take us to the airport. I was uneasy. Porter and Madame Rozinko held a hurried conversation. Then Madame Rozinko looked at me. Her customary gaiety had disappeared. Now her mouth was hard and her eyes were grim.

"Who are you, what do you do, and who sent you?" she asked rapidly.

"Who are you, what do you do, and who sent *you*?" I retorted.

For a minute, it looked like she would explode with anger; then suddenly she smiled. Next, she threw back her head and laughed. It was a marvelous, infectious peal of mirth. Porter joined in. Soon the three of us were howling with laughter at the incongruous situation. Madame Rozinko

7

laughed so hard that tears were streaming down her face. She asked no more questions.

As we neared the airport, Madame Rozinko handed me her card. "When you are in Bucharest again," she said, "please call on me. I want to get better acquainted with a man as bold as you are."

When we got to the terminal, the chauffeur pulled the car right up to the main entrance. After opening the doors for us, he took the luggage in ahead. Porter stiffened as our little group neared the customs lines.

"Get ready," he whispered to me. "Do your stuff." Again he was pale and breathing shallowly. He knew that if I were caught, he, too, would be in trouble. Just as the customs agents reached for my bags, Madame Rozinko intervened.

"Don't open those," she ordered. "I okay them personally." She grabbed a piece of chalk from the startled customs agent and marked a symbol on my suitcases. Then she scrawled the same mark on Porter's bags. I don't know whether she was aware of the contents of my bags or not.

We left Madame Rozinko at customs and moved off down the hall.

"That was incredible!" Porter said. "Look, here's my card. It has my private Telex number. If you are ever apprehended, arrested, or detained for questioning, send me an SOS. I have connections with British Intelligence. I will do my best to see that you're released. When you call, use this code name. He handed me a little card. "It means 'love' in Romanian. I'll know who you are. You are the man who told me that God so loved the world."

Suddenly Porter's eyes filled with tears. His voice broke. He was openly weeping as he continued. "After what I saw just now, I have to believe in God. I know now that there is a God and that He is the One who got you through the customs. I would like to accept Jesus as my Savior."

8

Weeping unabashedly, Porter prayed his way to Christ. Still weeping, he headed for his plane, almost stumbling as he walked. Miraculously, none of the guards seemed to notice his strange behavior.

I never saw Alec Porter again. He boarded a flight to Vienna; I took an Aeroflot jet to Moscow. But several years later, back in America, I ran across a CIA executive and mentioned Porter's real name to him. The CIA man knew all about him. My suspicions had been correct. Alec Porter really was a spy. And who knows? By now, he too may be a spy for God.

Chapter Two
Still Kicking

It's funny how I ended up doing what I'm doing. When I was a boy, it never occurred to me that I'd grow up to be a smuggler and, occasionally, a spy, and I had some pretty wild imaginings even for a boy. I wanted to be Zorro, I wanted to be Superman, and I wanted to be a spaceman—like Flash Gordon. But although I enjoyed my games of warfare and intrigue, in my heart I realized that they were only fantasies. Back then, all my adventures were make-believe.

I was born on a hot, muggy day in August—and in Galveston, Texas, August can get pretty hot and muggy. My mother remembers the day quite vividly. She was in a lot of pain, her legs swollen with phlebitis. I was so big—and mamma was so slightly built—that towards the end it was difficult for her to move around, even on the days her legs didn't hurt too badly. Mamma is four foot nine, and at the time of her marriage she weighed only ninety-nine pounds.

She was impatient for me to be born. I was her first child,

and for days she'd been cooped up in the tiny apartment she and pappa had rented near Galveston's sea wall. Mamma is an active person, but the doctors had told her that she would have to stay quiet most of the time, sitting or lying as much as possible, since a blood clot could come loose from one of the veins in her legs and reach her heart or lungs. So mamma sat patiently.

Before coming to this country with her father and two older brothers, mamma lived till she was eight in a little stone house perched high on a rocky Greek hillside near Tripolis. She was raised by my grandfather, a learned, graybearded Greek Orthodox priest who spoke six languages. Grandfather Petros was very close to the Lord he served.

The day I was born, mamma was thinking of Greece, thankful that she was in a country where modern medical facilities were readily available. Had she stayed in Greece, she would probably have had to depend on a midwife to deliver the baby, and it would have been delivered at home. Mamma had grown up in a primitive, poverty-stricken area. The home of her childhood had had two stories: the lower one had been a stable, and the upper one had held the living quarters. Food had been cooked under a canvas canopy jutting out from the wall of the house. The house had been built into a hill; the kitchen was in the back, adjoining the living quarters. Water had been supplied by a pump; sanitary facilities were provided by an outhouse.

In spite of the rugged beauty of her hillside home, mamma was glad she had come to America, where she could have modern plumbing and up-to-date medical care. In her condition, mamma wanted the best medical care available.

Mamma's reveries were interrupted by the onset of her pains. Quickly, she called my father, who rushed her to John Sealy Hospital.

In the corridor, pappa pressed mamma's hand, whispering words of endearment and encouragement in Greek as the white-coated attendants prepared to wheel her away. Mamma summoned up a last bit of strength and blew pappa a kiss as she vanished down the hall. Then, for hours, pappa sat in the waiting room hoping and praying.

Finally, pappa looked up to see Dr. Cook in the doorway, beckoning him out into the corridor. Pappa hurried out into the hall, feeling so nervous that it was hard for him to breathe.

"Mr. Panos," Dr. Cook said, "I have bad news for you."

Pappa's heart sank. Was it his wife, or the baby? He was afraid to ask. Before he could, Dr. Cook continued, speaking quickly now.

"I don't think we are going to be able to save both your wife and the baby. She is in great distress. Her pains are very strong and the baby is large. We may be able to save them both, but the probability is that we will not—"

Dr. Cook looked at pappa as though he were asking him a question. He didn't understand. The enormity of the news had stunned him. Before he had time to recover, Dr. Cook was putting the awful question into words. "What would you like me to do? Do you want me to save your wife or the baby?"

Pappa was dazed by grief. It was hard for him to think. He didn't know what mamma would have wanted him to do. They had wanted this baby so much! But mamma was his wife. They could always try again. Maybe in a year or two, after mamma had recovered. He looked at Dr. Cook through tears. "Save the mother. Save my wife."

Dr. Cook turned and hurried back toward the delivery room, knowing what my father had no way of knowing that there would probably never be another baby for my parents. It was to be this child or none at all.

13

Mamma gave birth shortly after Dr. Cook returned from talking to my father. Immediately, she was wheeled to her room. In the delivery room I remained, still and blue. Oxygen hadn't yet found its way into my lungs. Dr. Cook tried for a while to get me to breathe, then gave me up for dead.

Back in her room, mamma lay exhausted, staring at the ceiling fan and praying. She had hoped for a boy. She knew that the baby had been a boy. But she also knew that he hadn't been breathing when they wheeled her from the room.

Suddenly—right in the ceiling fan—mamma saw a vision of Jesus. How kind He looked! In her heart, she heard His voice. "Your son is not going to die. He will live and be a blessing. You are not to name him Petros after your father. He is to be named Christos."

The words sank indelibly into mamma's heart. She repeated them over and over again to herself, cherishing each word, savoring the precious message. Then she called for pappa and told him what she had seen. Both of them knew it would take a miracle to save my life.

My parents needed a miracle, and a miracle is what they got. Still in the operating room, Dr. Cook decided to make one last attempt to save my life. He put a small rubber suction hose into my mouth and drew on it. Aha! He nodded to himself, satisfied. The tube was filled with mucus. No wonder the child couldn't breathe. He drew again. The mucus which had blocked my throat and lungs came free. The doctor upended me. *Slap!* He tried again. *Slap!* The doctor smiled as I cried and kicked.

As my father likes to tell it, before Dr. Cook set to work , "Christos was lying on the shelf like a brick. But suddenly he began to kick, and he's still kicking today!"

Soon after bringing me home from the hospital, my parents had me christened. When the christening day arrived,

14

Grandfather Petros came to the Greek Orthodox church to pray the blessing of God on me. He stood at the front of the ornate church near the carved bowl of water, graybearded and robed in black, proud to be a grandfather and conscious, as a priest, that an eternal soul was being entrusted to him for baptism.

Carefully and reverently, Grandfather Petros started the baptismal ceremony, exorcising any evil spirits that might be present, blessing the baptismal water, and anointing me with the "oil of gladness." Next he dipped me in the baptismal font three times as I squalled and kicked. Then came the "Baptism of the Holy Spirit." Anointing me with oil, Grandfather Petros prayed for me to receive the experience that the Church was given on the day of Pentecost. Setting my senses apart for the use of God, Grandfather Petros anointed me on ears, eyes, nose, lips, and hands.

"The seal of the gift of the Holy Spirit, Amen," he began intoning. "The seal of the gift of the Holy Spirit, Amen. The seal of the gift of the Holy Spirit—"

As he held me, grandfather smiled. My mother had told him about the vision of Christ that she'd had earlier. How else could she explain why they were no longer planning to name the baby after him?

"And this," grandfather thought, "this is the child who would have borne my name. Ah, well, if I have to play second fiddle, at least they're naming the baby after the One Person I don't mind playing second fiddle to!"

Mentally, Grandfather Petros shook himself. The people were waiting. A celebration had been planned following the service. "Father," he prayed aloud, "may everything this child touches be blessed of God."

"And Father," he whispered, "make this child a bishop of the Greek Orthodox church."

My grandfather must have prayed long and hard for me,

and it's a good thing that he did. I've had a lot of narrow escapes in my time, and who knows whether the prayers of my grandfather are what decided the outcome?

The first narrow escape of my life—not counting my miracle birth—came when I was still in diapers. My parents had moved to a new apartment near Galveston Bay shortly after I was christened. In the new apartment, my parents could hear the sound of the waves breaking on the shore, and at night a cool sea breeze made the new apartment comfortable. For the sweltering daytime heat, they had only one small fan which looked like a refugee from a junk shop. My parents had bought the fan secondhand because they didn't want to spend money for nonessentials, and to them, new furnishings were nonessential. They were saving for the day when my father could buy a cafe and go into business for himself.

The fan my parents bought had a frayed, soiled cord. It had lost its guard, and one of its blades was slightly bent. The paint was peeling and spots of rust showed through here and there, but it ran dependably. Knowing that overheated babies tend to cry and fret, my parents used the fan to cool me as I played and slept.

Mamma has often told me about the day when she wished they had never bought that fan.

"You weren't very old, Christos," she said. "You were still wearing diapers. You were even too young to crawl. I had put you down on the couch, and I had put the little fan on the floor near the couch, so you'd stay nice and cool while I did my housework. I left the room for just a minute, but as I was coming back in I saw you fall off the couch. You hit the back of the fan and knocked it over. It began to roll over and fall straight at your stomach. It looked like it was about to cut you open. I cried out to Mary. 'Mary! Save my son!' And suddenly, a pillow came off the opposite corner of the couch, flew through the air, and went straight into the blades of the fan. It stopped the fan. There was no reason for the pillow to come off the couch like that. It looked as if an invisible hand had just picked it up and pushed it straight into the blades."

Mamma didn't cry out in the name of Jesus, she cried out in the name of Mary. Years later, when I came to the Lord, that confused me. I said, "Lord, You know that You haven't exalted the name of Mary above the name of Jesus."

He said, "I know it; but, son, I use what I have."

Today, my mother would cry out in the name of Jesus. Back then, she didn't know she could do that, so she used what she had. And I'm glad it worked. Otherwise, I might not be here today.

Chapter Three
Christos Anesti

Mamma remembers me as a good boy. Her definition of a "good boy" is that, as she puts it, "You always loved your mamma." She's right—I did. We were a close-knit family, and although my parents worked long, hard hours at the cafe and I was sometimes lonely at night when I was put to bed and left home alone in the apartment, I was always sure of my parents' love for me.

Throughout my boyhood, my parents told me tales of Greece, a seagirt land of steep, emerald hillsides dropping down to crashing ocean waves, a land of stunted oaks and wiry shrubs where wild flowers carpet the sea slopes in the spring, goats gambol on the cliffs, and farmers coax olives and other fruits from tree-planted terraces hand-hewn into the sides of mountains.

Mamma left Greece with my Grandfather Petros and her two older brothers when she was eight; pappa left when he was in his early teens. Pappa's father had died and left him the family business—a store and a restaurant—in preference to his mother and his older brothers. Pappa's inheritance wasn't much by American standards, but it was big enough to make him one of the wealthiest men in his little village.

Pappa's brothers were angered and envious, and to make matters worse, pappa's mother remarried, and his new step-father didn't like him either. To pappa, home life was miserable and full of hazards. He decided the inheritance wasn't worth it; he would make his own fortune. So pappa stowed away on a boat bound for America.

When I was a boy, pappa used to tell me about how he came to this country. "I had big plans, Christos," he would say. "I said to myself, 'I will go to this land I have heard of, this America.' And so I sneaked down to the harbor and asked where each ship was heading. When I found one that was going to New York, I slipped on board and stowed away. Nobody seemed to notice me. Maybe they thought I was traveling with someone else, because I was just thirteen at the time.

"I was happy and excited—until we got out to sea. When the ship hit the open water, it wasn't long before I knew I had made a big mistake. I wished I had never heard of America and had never left home. I wasn't homesick and I didn't miss my mamma. No, Christos, I was sorry I had left because I was seasick all the way across!"

When pappa landed in New York, on solid ground at last, it was with little money and no English. Mamma's family fared better when they came over. For one thing, they had relatives here already. For another, Grandfather Petros knew six languages, and one of them was English. For several years—after leaving Greece and before coming to America—grandfather's learning had enabled him to find work all over Europe as a tutor. Pappa, on the other hand, had no relatives in America. The only way he could communicate was through sign language.

"To buy food, Christos," pappa would tell me, "I would have to point to what I wanted, or draw a picture of it in the air, or use sign language. I always used to be able to get chicken without any trouble at all. I would flap my arms and hop up and down, cackling and crowing."

When I was four, war came to Europe and caught Greece in its crossfire. Mussolini sent troops into Greece in 1940, demanding that Premier Alexander Papagos let him use Greek bases. Papagos refused.

The Greek army was small and ill-equipped. Despite these disadvantages, the Greeks forced the Italians back across the border. By December, Greece had driven out the invaders and conquered much of Albania. Not to be outdone, Mussolini went to Hitler for help and Hitler responded with thousands of highly trained German soldiers equipped with the latest in artillery, tanks, and aircraft. Greece fought bravely, but the goose-stepping German soldiers had the advantage in both numbers and munitions. On April 6, 1941, Greece surrendered to the armies of Hitler's Third Reich.

Greece was occupied after her surrender by Italian, German, and Bulgarian troops who foraged off the land. Unfortunately, only about one-fourth of Greece's rocky, mountainous land is arable and there simply wasn't enough food to feed the invaders and the Greeks as well.

The situation soon became desperate. Many of the very old and the very young starved to death. It was a time of great suffering and privation, but despite the hardships, bands of Greek guerrillas continued to harass the occupying forces.

Here in America the Greek community rallied around its homeland, raising funds to save as many of the starving Greek children as possible. Christy Mitchell, an older cousin of mine, wrote a column called "The Beachcomber" for the Galveston newspaper. Eager to do whatever he could to help, he worked up a publicity program for Greek war relief. In this program, he used a picture of me as a symbol of the starving Greek children. For Christy's campaign, mamma sewed a traditional Greek soldier's costume for me to wear.

"Here, Christos," mamma said, "put this on. This is a warrior's costume. Greek heroes have worn this costume since the time when Alexander the Great conquered the world, a long, long time before pappa or I was born. Now you are going to be a little hero, too. Your picture will be in the newspaper, and when the people see the picture of the brave little Greek soldier, they will send money to feed the children in Greece who don't have any food to eat. Stand still, while I show you how to wear these."

Mamma dressed me in the soldier outfit with its short-skirted *fostanella*, and draped its short cape, the *gelecki*, as though it had been tossed around my shoulder. A little soldier's cap sat proudly on my head, and on my feet were the traditional *charoukia*, made of real goatskin. I was excited and proud as the news photographer took my picture.

The publicity campaign was a great success; thousands of dollars were raised for the starving children. In addition the Greeks in Galveston collected used clothing and blankets and shipped them off to Greece, often slipping silver dollars into the pockets of the clothes.

Pearl Harbor came and went, but pappa worked on in the Snug Harbor Cafe. Early in 1942, he made a big step forward: he and mamma went to work for Uncle Sam Keres, who had just bought the T&P Cafe in Fort Worth, Texas. Uncle Sam was still a bachelor, and he needed help running the cafe.

We moved to Fort Worth and found an apartment near the T&P Cafe. It was a rough part of town, and the cafe looked no different, but the food was good. Pappa and Uncle Sam would serve a regular breakfast and lunch, with mainly short orders at night. Because of the cafe's location, many of its customers were unsavory characters. I grew to know gamblers, crooks, pimps, and prostitutes at an early age. I thought the bad guys were exciting, and I enjoyed listening in on the conversations of people I considered to be men and women of the world.

The cafe had other benefits, as well. My parents let me have all the candy and sweets I wanted. If I wanted candy or gum or a piece of pie, I just went in and took it without asking. I must have run off the extra calories, because I never got fat.

I used to spend a lot of time in that cafe, especially since one of my chores was washing the dishes in the afternoons. Six days a week my family ate at the cafe; the seventh, Sunday, the cafe was closed.

Sunday was important in our family, not only because the cafe was closed, but also because that was the day we went to church. To a Greek Orthodox, church is more than a religion, it's a way of life. Being the daughter of a priest, mamma naturally made sure I went to church on Sundays. Pappa would go, too. After church, there was often a dinner in the church hall next door. After we ate, the women would gossip and the men would drink beer and play card games. Sometimes, somebody would play a record of Greek music and we'd dance the Greek dances, holding hands in a semi-circle, watching as the leader would suddenly leap high in the air, clicking his heels, then drop in a knee bend to slap the floor and rise again, whirling in counterpoint to the rest of us. In Greece, the men and the women dance in different circles, but here in America, we all mixed in together.

Our family worked too hard to socialize much, but we were Greek, and the Greeks in Fort Worth were very close in those days. To make sure we stayed that way, all of the boys went to the Greek Orthodox church twice a week after school. There we learned what it meant to be Greek. The priest taught us not only Greek religion but Greek culture as well. We learned about Homer, Socrates and Aristotle; and we learned about the great Greek heroes like Alexander the Great and Athanasius Diacos, a hero of the War of 1812.

"Diacos," the priest lectured, "means deacon. Athanasius Diacos happened to be a deacon of the Greek Orthodox church, and that's how he got his nickname.

"Tony Diacos was one of the heroes of the war in which the Greeks threw off the Turkish yoke. He was so brave that even the Turks admired him. They wanted to spare his life. They wanted him to join their side. They wanted him to become a Turk, to become a Muslim. At first the Turks asked him politely; later on they tortured him. And do you know what our brave Athanasius said, children?"

We knew. "I was born a Greek, I will die a Greek. I was born a Christian, I will die a Christian," we chorused, thrills running through our hearts.

"That's right. He refused to become a Muslim. As a result, they tortured him. They put him on a spit and barbecued him, and as they did, they pleaded with him to become a Turk, to give up Jesus Christ, to join them and save his life. But our brave Athanasius would not give in. He died a martyr."

Our hearts raced to the tales the priest told, stories of great Greek heroes down through the centuries, bravely winning out against great odds. We hoped we would grow up to be as brave as Tony Diacos.

In our community, it was an honor to be a Greek. Greeks were cultured people who had been civilized centuries before the birth of Christ. And Greece had never really been defeated. Not even by the Germans. What happened during World War II, we told ourselves, was that Greece had sacrificed herself, giving America time to prepare for war.

Greece had been heroic and brave, standing to the last against insurmountable odds for the sake of her allies—and then harassing the enemy to the end by means of guerrilla warfare.

Easter, not Christmas, is the biggest religious holiday for Greeks. It is the most important holy day to the Greek Orthodox because there is a strong emphasis on the Resurrection in the Greek Orthodox church. All the events of Christ's betrayal, passion, crucifixion, burial, and resurrection are relived day by day in the Great Week services, and all Greek Orthodox are expected to attend.

As a boy, I used to love the Easter service. Other services might seem long and boring to a boy my age, but the Easter service was very dramatic. The church was darkened, all the lights were out, and everybody stood in front of the church with an unlighted candle. Suddenly, the priest would appear on the threshold. He, too, would carry a candle, but his would be lit, symbolizing the fact that Jesus is the light of the world.

The priest would chant, "Come forward and receive the light from the unsetting light—" and everybody would eagerly crowd forward to get a light. When everybody's candle was brightly burning, the priest would intone the account of the Resurrection from the Gospel of Mark. He would do this outside, still on the doorstep of the church. At the end of the account of the Resurrection, the priest would lead the congregation in singing *Christos Anesti: Christ is Risen. Christos Anesti*, the great paschal refrain, would be sung by the congregation over and over again in waves, picking up a crescendo, building up momentum, a great swelling wave of triumph in Jesus Christ, communicating a glad spirit of joy so that even an unregenerate little boy could feel something of the sense of victory.

Chapter Four
Tears Like Glass

Even though Easter was exciting, it wasn't enough excitement for a red-blooded little boy. I had a vivid imagination and used it to make my own excitement when none was forthcoming in day-to-day events.

I remember one time I was in the kitchen of the T&P Cafe. Pappa was out, and I was alone in back. I was supposed to be washing dishes—and I did wash some, at first.

Pappa's chef's hat was lying on the chopping block. It was irresistible. I tied an apron around my middle and put the tall white hat on my head: it was clean and white and smelled of starch. Suddenly, I was a great chef, like pappa. I extracted a large roast from the refrigerator and plopped it down on the well-scarred chopping block. Sinking a large fork firmly in the meat, I pulled out one of the carving knives from the rack on the side of the butcher block and began to carve.

This was my first attempt and it was a disaster. Instead of large, even slices of beef, the roast became wedges and hunks and shreds. I kept right on. I was determined to get the hang of it.

Suddenly, I heard a howl of anguish. "Christos! What are you doing?"

Pappa was back. He clutched the sides of his head as he looked at the remains of the roast.

"Oh, no," he moaned. "My beautiful roast. Ruined." Then he turned to me. "Christos," he shouted, "look what you have done!"

I didn't look—I ran. I abandoned pappa's chef's hat to its rightful owner and sprinted through the swinging doors into the cafe. He followed close behind—too close. The swinging doors caught him on the rebound. Then he really started speaking Greek!

With pappa running after me, I dashed out the front door of the cafe and ran down the street. As I ran, I abandoned my chef's role. I took the white apron and fastened it around my neck. Suddenly, I was Zorro, the caped crusader. No one ever catches Zorro, and besides I was wearing brand-new tennis shoes. Everybody knows that tennis shoes make little boys run at least ten times faster. But pappa caught me at the corner. Puffing hard, he walked me back to the cafe, pinching me on the seat as we went. The rest of the afternoon was all work and no play. Pappa kept a watchful eye on me, and made sure I did as I was told. The shreds of roast became a very high-class hash.

Irrepressible, I lived in play. The kids on our block would take their rubber guns and wooden swords and foray into adjoining neighborhoods to ambush the "enemies" living there. When we weren't playing war games, I had a friend, Jay Weinstein, who was the deaf mute to my Zorro. Zorro was my favorite hero.

Jay and I had a secret hideout in Jay's garage that you entered by a separate door. Zorro's horse was also stabled there, looking suspiciously like a bicycle to less romantic eyes.

I had assembled a Zorro outfit—wooden sword, cape, and mask—and cached it in the hideout, near my "horse," ready for use. When Jay was imperiled by the other children in their games of cops and robbers or cowboys and Indians, I would slip away, put on my Zorro outfit, climb on the bicycle, and race to the rescue. Zorro always arrived in the nick of time, carving his trademark—a snazzy (and in my case imaginary) "Z"—on the bad guys at the end of each adventure.

Like Zorro, I always rescued the good guy in the nick of time. Then, as fast as possible, I would return to the hideout, slip off my costume, and innocently rejoin the other children. They all knew who Zorro was, but I never admitted my part in the adventure, any more than Zorro did in the movie serials we all enjoyed.

Being Zorro wasn't always the easiest thing in the world. One Sunday, mamma had the table all set for dinner with her best white tablecloth. As I waited for Sunday dinner to be ready, I played Zorro with a little fencing sword I had been given. A little ball was fastened on its tip, so it was safe for me to play with, but although it had neither edge nor point, it made a very satisfactory *whish* as I slashed it through the air.

As I played, the table became the enemy hideout. Sneaking up on it, I engaged in a heated battle with the imaginary bad guys. Soon, they were defeated. I was elated: it was time to carve my "Z" for Zorro, to show that I had been there. There was only one small problem: Zorro always carved his "Z" in blood. I had no blood handy, but I had seen some red paint around. As mamma cooked, I quickly got the paint can. Dipping the tip of my sword in the thick red fluid, I left my "Z" right on mamma's Sunday tablecloth.

Soon, Zorro suffered a humiliating defeat at the hands of

the enemy. To add insult to injury, Zorro, like Samson, suffered his downfall at the hands of a woman.

"Christos! My best tablecloth!" mamma shouted. "Just wait! You are really going to get it."

I didn't know what was worse: the fact that mamma had discovered Zorro's real identity or the fact that she was running for her switch. All too quickly, she returned. In the duel that followed, Zorro's flashing, red-tipped sword was no defense against the blows rained down upon various portions of his anatomy. I was glad my friend Jay Weinstein couldn't see me now!

I was humiliated. I sulked all day. That night, I couldn't sleep. I got out of bed and went to the living room to brood. I was dressed only in my pajamas, so I took mamma's coat out of the closet. Mamma was very proud of that coat: it was made of real fur. It had cost $1,000, which was even more money back then than it is today.

As I huddled in mamma's coat, I got an idea. I would get revenge on mamma for the defeat I'd suffered at her hands that afternoon. A fire was smoldering on the grate, and I decided to burn mamma's coat in it. I went to the fireplace, but suddenly my feat of derring-do seemed too horrible to contemplate. I loved my mamma. Torn between my love and my desire for revenge, I fell asleep.

When I awoke, I had accomplished by accident what I had not had the nerve to accomplish by design. A sleeve of mamma's coat had fallen in the fireplace and most of the coat was a smoldering mess of ashes. I was unhurt.

I decided to put on a brave face. I got my sword and made a tremendous "Z" from the ashes of mamma's coat. Then I left the living room and crept into bed. I was sure that my parents wouldn't connect their innocent little Chrissy with whomever had done a dastardly deed like burning mamma's coat. But they did.

"George! George!" shrieked mamma from the living room. "Just look what Christos has done to my fur coat. What will be the end of this Zorro stuff of his?"

Quickly, I headed for safety. I leaped over the side of our porch and ran down the street. I was sure that pappa, old and fat, would be unable to follow me, but I was wrong again. He jumped right after me, and caught me only about a block away. Puffing and shouting, he removed his belt. Shouting angrily in Greek, he hit me with it all the way back home. This time it was total defeat. All the people on the block had seen me, including my friend, Jay.

An incident that should have ended my life of crime forever occurred when I was nine years old, in the summer of 1944. I had been helping my father at the cafe, but the breakfast rush was over. He would not need me again till lunch. So I decided to go over to my uncle's business, Peters Brothers Hats on Houston Street.

On the way over, I stopped at McCrory's dime store. After the Texas sun, it was cool and dark inside.

I headed straight for the toys. Nobody paid much attention to me as I wandered along the counters, playing with the guns and cars. But they were old stuff, not very interesting. Suddenly, I came upon a new display. Lead soldiers! I walked over to the counter where they were piled, separated from the other toys by thick glass dividers on either side. I picked one up. He was heavier than I expected, and looked like a real soldier, poised about to shoot. I picked up another one: he was standing at attention, stiff and straight. Soon, a battle was raging on the toy counter.

I don't know how long the lead soldiers battled on that counter, but suddenly I became aware of an interior battle as well. I wanted those soldiers so badly! I felt in my pocket. There was a little money, but not enough. I held a soldier in my hand, wanting him so badly my heart nearly broke. I didn't have enough money and I knew it was no use asking mamma or pappa for it. They would probably yell at me for asking—angry words about rent and prices and the value of thrift.

Then I made my decision. I grabbed a sack from a shelf under the counter and started scooping it full of soldiers. I filled the sack, turned, walked out of the store, and back toward the cafe. No one seemed to notice my departure.

I took the long way around to get back to the cafe, passing City Hall and the Catholic church by the park, admiring one of the soldiers I had taken out of the sack.

As I passed the park, I looked across the street. An enormous man—twenty-five feet tall or more—was standing on a huge rock. He was looking at me. I knew the man was Jesus. He was crying.

"Oh, no!" I thought. "He saw me steal the soldiers!"

The moment I saw Him, I felt sorry for what I'd done. I dropped the soldier back in the sack. Jesus just kept looking at me. He was dazzling, solid white. The tears on His cheeks looked like glittering hunks of glass.

"He's looking at me. He can't believe I would do a thing like that. He's crying because I stole the soldiers!" I was crying too.

I can't explain what happened then. It was like I zoomed across the street. Suddenly, I was face to face with Him. He was looking right at me—right into me—right through me. I ran.

I ran as fast as I could go, not slowing down as I neared the cafe. I burst in the front door, slamming it behind me.

"Mamma! Mamma!" I shouted in Greek. "Mamma! Mamma! I saw the Lord! I saw Jesus Christ!"

She was startled. "What did you say?" she asked.

"I saw Jesus. I saw the Lord. He saw me take the soldiers.

He saw me steal them from McCrory's. Will He forgive me? Will He forgive me? I'm sorry, I'm sorry." I burst into tears.

It was almost lunchtime, and the cafe was nearly full. I had been shouting in Greek, but the commotion embarrassed mamma. "Simmer down, Christos, simmer down. Don't be crazy," she said.

Pappa came out of the kitchen. "What's going on here?" he asked. "What's all the commotion?"

"I saw Jesus," I told him. "He saw me steal the soldiers!"

"He's imagining things," mamma said. "He didn't see anything."

"Yes, I did!" I insisted. "Yes, I did! I saw Jesus! He was big and white, and He was crying because He'd seen me steal the soldiers."

It was obvious that my parents didn't believe me. "Come on, I'll show you where I saw Him," I told them, tugging at mamma's hand.

Everybody was watching by then, obviously wondering what was going on. Both mamma and pappa agreed to go, which was unusual because they almost never left the cafe together; one of them always had to watch the cash register. Neither of them even waited to remove their aprons.

Still clutching the sack of soldiers, I led them back to the park. Well, almost to the park.

"You go around and see if He's still there," I told mamma as we got to the corner. "I'll come if He's gone."

Mamma and pappa went to the corner. I watched them intently, trying to tell from their retreating backs whether the Man was there or not. They disappeared, then reappeared, motioning me to follow. I edged up to the corner and peeked around. The coast was clear. No Man.

"See, you didn't see nothing," mamma said.

"Yes, I did," I responded. "He was standing right over there. It was Jesus."

33

We crossed the street into the park and looked around. They decided I had probably seen a statue. They took me to the Catholic church next door where there were several statues.

"That must be what you saw," mamma said, pointing to a statue of Mary and the baby Jesus.

"No, mamma. I wasn't in here. Besides, it wasn't any baby I saw. I saw a Man—a big Man. He was crying."

"Mamma!" pappa burst out. "The cash register!" Suddenly remembering that they had left the cafe untended, my parents rushed me back. I was very uneasy at lunch. I could hardly eat. I kept seeing Jesus, and the glittering tears on his enormous cheeks.

Jesus was crying for me.

Chapter Five
Kill the Greek!

The afternoon after I stole the soldiers, mamma and pappa decided that I would have to be taught a lesson, and they chose my Uncle Tom to administer it. Uncle Tom was the head of mother's side of the family, and was the wealthiest of my relatives. He was from the old country, where permissiveness was unheard of. To indicate the seriousness with which he viewed my crime, Uncle Tom came to the cafe to lecture me himself.

"Christos," Uncle Tom began, "your mamma and pappa told me what you have done. That was a terrible thing to do. How can I face my friends, when they hear about this? I have a lot of friends in this town. When they hear what you have done, they won't even want to be seen with me. Stealing is awful; nobody likes a thief—"

Uncle Tom's voice droned on and on, mouthing platitudes about the value of honesty and the family's good name. I hardly heard him. It was all too apparent that Uncle Tom was worried more about his own reputation than he was about my moral character.

"And of course," he continued, "you will have to return all the soldiers that you stole. You will have to take them back yourself. I have already phoned the manager that you are coming."

Well, that was okay with me, I thought. I didn't even want the stupid soldiers anymore. I didn't want to keep them around. I was sorry that I had ever seen them.

Uncle Tom went with me and so did a cousin of mine. Uncle Tom was stiff and disapproving, but my cousin was more understanding. I attributed this difference to the fact that my cousin was not from the old country like Uncle Tom. And besides, my cousin was younger, closer to my age.

I was convinced that the older adults got, the less they remembered how it felt to be young. An old man like Uncle Tom, I reasoned, couldn't possibly be expected to sympathize with a young person my age.

When we got to McCrory's, Uncle Tom waited outside on the sidewalk. My cousin accompanied me as I went inside to see the manager. I was afraid, but my fears proved to be groundless.

"You must be Chris Panos," said the manager. "I've been expecting you. I'm very happy that you have decided to return the soldiers that you took. It takes a big man to admit when he's been wrong."

"Here they are," I told him, handing him the bag. "I am sorry I took them." I *was*, too, but I knew that whether I was sorry or not, I would have had to say so. Uncle Tom would be checking with the manager later on that afternoon. "And, sir," I concluded, "I promise you that I will never do it again."

I kept my promise to the manager of McCrory's. There was just too much other trouble to get into! Although the vision of Jesus shook me at the time, I quickly managed to forget it.

Instead of reforming, I began to get into more and more mischief as time went by. I lived in a bad part of town, and I had a lot of free time to myself. My parents worked long hours at the cafe, and even when I was actually present there at the cafe with them, they were much too busy working to notice what I was getting into. Often, however, instead of being with my parents at the cafe, I'd be down the street somewhere, investigating the back rooms and pool halls that infested our neighborhood.

I was still a small boy, but I had big ears and I caught on fast. Years before I needed to know about such things, I had received a thorough course in sex education from remarks dropped by the waitresses and customers in the cafe. It wasn't a wholesome education. A lot of it was overheard from the conversation of pimps and prostitutes, who had a rather commercial outlook on the subject. But I had bad influences all around me: in that neighborhood, no one was immune.

In addition to the pimps, the prostitutes, and the gangsters that frequented the neighborhood establishments, there were my own playmates and my cousin Theodore. Theodore was ten years older than I, and he helped show me the ways of the world. Not that I needed much showing. I already knew how to steal and to cheat at cards; I knew how to deal from either end of the deck with equal facility; and I knew how to spoon the slot machines for spending money.

Even before I learned how to spoon them, I had been fascinated by the one-armed bandits at the back of the T&P Cafe. I had seen people hit the right combination and coins would just pour out. I decided that I, too, was going to hit the jackpot. To play the slot machines, I stole dimes and quarters from the cash register.

I pulled the handles of those old one-armed bandits time and time again, but I rarely got any return on my "investment." Finally, I noticed that an occasional customer had a different method of proceeding. One of them, years older than I, was a friend of mine.

"What are those?" I asked him.

He looked at the strange devices in his hands and then at me. He must have decided either that I could be trusted or else that it was too late for secrecy, because he threw caution to the winds.

"These are spoons," he said.

I watched as he fitted the devices into the machines. With the spoons inserted, the machines came up three of a kind every time. My friend diplomatically gave me a portion of his illicit jackpot.

Soon, I obtained my own set of spoons. Thereafter, I had all the money I wanted, simply by spooning the machines. My cousin Theodore knew what I was doing.

"The police don't care if you steal from those machines," he explained. "They're illegal anyway. But be careful of the hoods—the men who put them in. They won't like it if they catch you stealing from them."

Burglarizing the illegal machines was even more exciting than trying to hit the jackpot. This time, I had real enemies: the hoods. I spooned machines all over the neighborhood, so the hoods wouldn't be too suspicious. I reasoned that they would catch on pretty quickly if the machines in the T&P Cafe were always empty, but if all the machines were empty on occasion, they might just assume that a lot of people had been hitting jackpots lately. Even if they knew something was wrong, I told myself, this way there wouldn't be anything to point to me. I was sure I couldn't be caught.

As I grew older, people stopped calling me Chris. Instead, they began to refer to me as the Greek. I suppose the nickname was inevitable: I was the only Greek in the crowd I ran with. I was still proud of my Greek heritage, but most

Kill the Greek!

Greeks are law-abiding people. I loved my relatives, but for friends, I found non-Greek hoodlums more exciting.

The crowd I ran with was not the crowd I knew from school—although I did participate in some activities with kids from school as well. I led a kind of double life: at school I was an honor student and a star on the track team; on the streets, I was a hoodlum, hanging out with a group of young thugs who were all much older than myself.

To maintain my status as a hoodlum, I was tough. I had to be. I was small for my age, and in rough neighborhoods, the smaller you are, the better you have to fight. With me, though, fighting was not just a matter of self-defense. It became a point of pride with me to be able to out-fight, out-drink, out-gamble, out-do anyone at anything. I was the Greek. I was beginning to have a reputation to maintain.

One of the things I prided myself upon was my ability to consume enormous amounts of alcohol. Then or later, it never occurred to me to question whether I was an alcoholic. To me, an alcoholic was someone who wanted to quit and couldn't. I never wanted to quit. Drinking was he-man stuff. I wanted to be a he-man.

The first time I got drunk, I was thirteen. My parents had a green, round-nosed 1948 Frazier, which I "borrowed" without their permission. A friend and I had planned a double date. With my friend and the two girls, I drove to Fort Worth's Forest Park. An older friend had bought a half-pint of whiskey for me; I planned to drink it all.

We sat in the car and talked, while I impatiently waited until I thought the time had come. I was trying to act casual: I wanted my friends to think I did this all the time. When the proper moment arrived, I brought out the whiskey. The girls were horrified; my friend said nothing.

"What are you worried about?" I asked them. "Drinking is nothing. There isn't anything to it." I held up the bottle.

"See this? I can drink it right down."

I broke the seal, opened the bottle, and started drinking. As I did, I nearly choked on the fumes. I hid my discomfort and took a long pull on the bottle. The whiskey burned my mouth and throat as I chug-a-lugged it down. In a few moments, I noticed that the street lights were beginning to look a little blurred. So was everything else, for that matter. When I tried to talk, I was surprised to find that I had to concentrate to do so. My tongue felt thick and clumsy. It was hard to articulate the words.

We left the car in the little parking area and went for a walk in the woods. I was having trouble with my balance. I don't remember how long we walked, but I do remember seeing some big, hairy tarantulas while we were there. I went back to the car and got my baseball bat out of the trunk. The girls looked scared and whispered to each other as I tried to hit the spiders, laughing and shouting. My aim was bad, so I didn't hit too many. The girls looked like they thought I'd hit them next.

"Please, Chris," one of them said. "Let's go home. It's awfully late. Our parents will be worried."

"Who cares about parents?" I said. But the girls begged and pleaded, so I agreed to go. As we headed down University Boulevard, I ran the Frazier into a bridge underpass. I dented in the rounded nose of the car and shook all of us up, but no one was hurt. The girls were more scared than ever.

As I grew, I was the toughest guy in a tough gang of kids. Tough as I was, however, one day I found a soft spot lurking beneath my hard exterior. I fell in love. Her name was Elizabeth. I thought she was just about the sweetest thing that I had ever seen. There was only one snag. I was not the only one enamored of Elizabeth, and she seemed unable or unwilling to decide between the two of us. My rival and I decided to settle the matter ourselves. We would have a fight, and the winner would continue to date her, while the other one would stay away.

We set a date for our fight, and somehow just about the whole high school heard about it. Both of us were class leaders, well-known and well-liked by the others. But Tom was more clean-cut than I was. While I spooned slot machines for spending money, Tom earned his honestly on a paper route.

The day before we were to have had our fight, Tom became an occupational fatality. He was delivering his papers when, somehow, he leaned a little bit too far out the door of his car, fell, and was killed.

The news of Tom's death shook the school. A few days later, we all turned out for the funeral. After that episode, Elizabeth and I both lost interest in each other. It had turned out to be just an infatuation.

That incident with Elizabeth had its effect, however. I had been tough before; now I turned tougher, hard and mean. By the time I was sixteen, I had grown a big, black moustache. I had a heavy beard and looked years older than my age. I faked identification to show that I was twenty-one, the legal drinking age in Texas. I searched out the roughest men and the toughest bars that I could find, looking for action. The Fort Worth hoods all knew me well. I called them by their first names, while they, in turn, watched me much the way an older brother watches a younger one. As far as they were concerned, the Greek was showing promise.

Fort Worth was a haven for gangsters in those days. The newspapers were filled with stories of gangland slayings, of bodies found in abandoned wells, of automobile dynamitings and shotgun murders. Prostitution and illegal gambling ran rampant. The gangs were looking for fresh young talent. With so much going on, there was a lot to be done, and not enough people to do it. Besides, the hoodlums had a way of running through personnel rather quickly. With that kind of turnover, they often needed replacements. So they kept an eye on me.

My life of crime nearly came to a quick halt one warm summer evening. I was out with a good friend of mine, Ricardo Vasquez. He was a Mexican and he was older than I was, but we spent a lot of time hanging out together. That night, we decided to go to a bar in his section of town. We went around to the front at first, drinking and smoking. It was pretty dull on that side, so we decided to go around back, where all the Mexicans drank. In those days, segregation was practiced for browns as well as blacks, but Ricardo was light enough and I was dark enough so that we could pass on either side as long as we were together. The Mexicans all knew I was Greek, but they considered me to be just another foreigner like themselves.

The back room of the bar was dimly lit, and full of smoke. Ricardo and I stood near the door for a moment, getting our eyes adjusted to the lack of light and listening to the Mexican songs blaring from the juke box. I was in an ugly mood and looking for a fight.

Ricardo and I stood at the bar for a while, talking about nothing much. I was standing next to a big Mexican who was older, heavier, and taller than I was. I watched him, waiting for a chance. It came. The Mexican started to lift his beer. I stepped to the side and "accidentally" bumped his arm. Beer spilled down the front of his shirt.

"What are you doing, punk?" the Mexican demanded. "I ought to cut your head off."

"Just try it, you fat slob. You haven't got the guts. The only guts you have are in that big spare tire of yours!"

His hand went for his knife. Before it got there, I slammed my beer bottle against his face, backhanded. I had expected to knock him down, but he just stood there. He shook his head and looked at me, probably deciding that I was crazy after all.

When the Mexican didn't go down, I knew I was in trouble. He grabbed his knife and I grabbed his arm. We wrestled across the bar, stumbled over some tables, and fell to the floor. I was not able to get the advantage. He was bigger and stronger than I was, and he was slippery with beer and sweat.

In the bar, everything came to a halt, even the juke box. We were the main event. The Mexicans yelled encouragement to my antagonist: "Kill the Grego! Kill the Grego!"

I got away from my opponent briefly and jumped on a platform in front of the plate glass window. He dove at me and we both went crashing through the glass.

As we fell through the glass onto the sidewalk, I felt a sharp stab of pain in my lower back. My back and trousers became warm and wet with blood. I thought I'd cut my back on the window. Then I saw the Mexican's knife. The edge of the switchblade was red with blood.

The Mexican sat on top of me. He was so heavy I could hardly breathe, and the wound made it painful to fight for breath. He held his knife loosely, expertly, the way a real knife fighter does. As I looked at him, he showed his gold-rimmed teeth in an evil smile.

"No guts, huh?" he commented. "Now, Greek, I'm just going to carve you up a little bit."

There was nothing I could do. My own switchblade was in my pocket and I couldn't get to it. He planned to play with me, to cut me up a little before he really hurt me—or killed me. I grabbed at his wrist. He laughed and pulled his arm back and up.

"I'm going to die," I thought incredulously. "I'm going to die!"

Suddenly, the picture of Jesus in the park flashed briefly

43

before my eyes. But I couldn't concentrate on it; I was watching the Mexican. Just as his knife started downward, Ricardo jumped from the doorway, kicking the knife out of his hand. As the knife flew away, Ricardo hit the Mexican with a beer bottle, knocking him off. "Come on, Chris," Ricardo shouted as he pulled me up. "Let's get out of here before they kill us both!"

We ran. Behind us, we could hear the shouts of the Mexicans in the bar. They were yelling for blood. We were careful where we went after that.

Soon after I graduated from high school, the big-time hoods began to take more notice of me. I started hanging around with them in their bars on Main and Houston and the Jacksboro Highway. At the time, it all seemed glamorous and exciting to me, but looking back I can see the sad part. Betty, for instance. Her father was a pimp. And Betty decided that she was going to be just like the girls who worked for her father. She didn't care how many boys she took on, and she was still in high school, just a kid. Bad as I was, things like that would bother me even then. I didn't understand myself. On the one hand I reveled in wrongdoing, on the other I was kind of softhearted.

Drugs weren't the big thing then that they are now, but the guys I hung out with dealt with them, and I would use them occasionally. I used to smoke a little pot sometimes, and I would take bennies to stay up, but the drug I used most was alcohol. I was just a real wrong sort of fellow. I was so bad that the hoods decided my kind of talent shouldn't be going to waste. They decided to hire me.

I was sitting in a bar on Houston Street, drinking beer, when their man approached me. The gangster settled himself on the barstool next to mine, motioning to the bartender.

"Hello, Greek," he said. The bartender set a stein of beer

in front of him. He took a sip and replaced it on the polished counter.

"Whatcha gonna do, kid?" the gangster asked me.

I knew what he meant, but I didn't answer.

"Either fight us or join us," he told me. "There's no middle ground. Either you're with us, or you're against us. There's no room in this town for freelancers. Make your choice, but make it quick." He had spoken quietly, but my ear caught the menacing tone in his voice. The gangsters didn't need to shout to get a point across: they could back up what they said with force. His point made, he got up and left, his stein of beer left barely tasted on the polished surface of the bar.

I decided to wait it out. While I was waiting, the papers were full of stories about another kid the gangsters had approached. He wasn't a friend of mine, but I had known him. He had thought he was going to oppose the organization. The hoods took him out into the country. There, they put a shotgun against his right bicep. One quick pull of the trigger, and the arm was gone. Next, they got the left arm. So much for the opposition. It eliminated him, and it served as a warning to all those who were thinking about bucking the gangsters.

I was still thinking about what I was going to do, when I went to a club with a pair of twins. One of the twins was a friend of mine, but I didn't know the other—and I didn't like him when he was introduced to me. He had just gone A.W.O.L. from the Marines. The tension must have been too much for him; that night, he started a fight that really wrecked that place. The whole bar erupted in a mass of flying chairs and broken bottles. Even the women joined in. When it was over, the club was a shambles.

I had waited too long to give the hoods an answer. After the fight, they thought that I had wrecked the club on purpose. They had seen me with the twins before the fight erupted and now they thought that I had put them up to it. The word went out: "Get the Greek!"

I planned to live to a ripe old age: I knew the time had come for me to leave Fort Worth. My parents and I decided I should go to Beaumont, where we had relatives. I packed my bag and got out.

Aside from my relatives, I knew no one in Beaumont, so my first social outing was a Greek Orthodox dance. They certainly had strange dances in Beaumont, I thought when I walked in.

"Where are all the girls?" I asked one of the boys standing nearby.

"They heard you were in town," he answered.

I thought he was joking. He wasn't. "Most of their parents have heard you had to leave Fort Worth. They were afraid to let the girls come—probably thought you'd snatch them from beneath their noses," he told me.

The parents of the girls weren't the only ones who were worried. My own parents were worried sick. They sold out their interest in the T&P Cafe and moved to Beaumont, where they had arranged to manage a cafe. It soon became apparent that the hoodlums were satisfied by my flight from town, but my parents didn't like the way I was acting. I had made no friends in Beaumont. I hadn't gotten a job. I lacked purpose.

Finally, my parents called me into the living room of our apartment.

"Christos," mamma asked, looking as though she was about to cry, "what are we going to do with you? What in the world are we ever going to do with you?"

I was silent. I saw no reason why they should do anything with me. It was my life and I intended to live it my own way. Besides, I thought, my parents were old. They just didn't know anything about the real world. Their minds were still in the old world. Cocky and adolescent, I thought I knew more about life than my parents did. We all sat in the living room, staring helplessly at one another.

Mamma looked at me. I was dressed in a flashy zoot suit, with my longish hair slicked back the way the gangsters wore it. As we sat there, her mind went back to the time of my birth. She remembered her vision, and the prophecy that I would be a blessing. I wasn't much of a blessing at present, to myself or to anybody else. Instead, Chris Panos was one big problem.

I didn't care. I didn't need my parents, or anybody. I would make it on my own. I reverenced God, but I just didn't feel as though He was relevant. In real life, you had to make it on your own.

That evening, though, I wasn't thinking about God. Instead, I was wondering what my parents were up to, with this family conference deal. I waited. Finally, pappa cleared his throat and broke the silence.

"Chris, your mamma and I have been talking about what to do with you. We think it would be better for you to move to Houston. You could work with your Uncle Steve."

I was surprised and pleased. I didn't like Beaumont very much, and I had made no friends there. Houston was a big town, with lots of opportunity. Uncle Steve was okay, too. Uncle Steve had been a wrestler: I could relate to him.

I agreed to move to Houston, and left the room. After I'd gone, mamma turned to pappa and said, "I hope Steve can handle him. He's so wild and different. I hope it will work out."

"Well," pappa told her, "after all, Steve Panos was a wrestler once. He's no softie. I think he can handle him."

I left for Houston eagerly, ready to impress the world.

Chapter Six
My Love Affair

Houston is a big city, a young city. Founded in 1836, it is now the largest city in the Southwest and the sixth largest in the nation. Although it is located fifty miles from the Gulf of Mexico and the huge Intracostal Canal, it is also an ocean port. Big ocean-going vessels reach the Port of Houston through a channel forty feet deep and four hundred feet wide which leads from the Gulf to the Turning Basin near the heart of the city. It was the opening of this channel in 1914 that marked the beginning of Houston's explosive growth. There were fortunes to be made in Houston and I planned to make me one.

I was encouraged in my ambitions by my Uncle Steve. Steve Panos was a self-made man. He wasn't rich, but he had attained an impressive affluence for a man who had started from scratch. By the time I went to work for him, he owned his own business, the Palace Boot Shop, located near Foley Brothers Department Store.

Uncle Steve was happy I had come to work for him. A

bachelor, he had no sons of his own. He was proud of his business, happy to have an opportunity to teach me the ropes, and determined to make a success out of me. That was okay with me. I was determined to become a success myself. My relatives, however, had had no way of knowing that, judging from my past escapades.

I got an apartment near Uncle Steve's and went to work. "Chris," he told me as he showed me around the shop, "there is no limit to what you can do. You can be anything you want to be. If you want it bad enough, you can be a millionaire. In this country, there is great opportunity.

"When I came to this country in 1919, Chrissy, I had nothing. I came to Houston without two nickles to rub together. First I shined shoes. Then I opened a little shoe-shine stand near here. With a lot of hard work and a little luck, I have built it into the Palace Boot Shop."

At first, I enjoyed my work with Uncle Steve. I was learning a lot. My work was hard and satisfying, but once I got home at night, I was at loose ends. I was used to going out every night, drinking and brawling and getting into trouble. Soon I met some local Houston boys who told me places to go and things to do. One night in the early fall, I went to a dance near where I lived. My friends had told me it would be a good place to meet girls. It was. I spent most of the night dancing with a girl named Earnestine Gardner.

For me, it was a case of love at first sight. Earnestine was the most beautiful girl I had ever seen. She had large hazel-brown eyes and soft brown hair with a reddish tint. She told me she managed a dress shop in Houston.

As we danced and talked, I learned more about her. Earnestine had come to Houston a year before from Laurel, Mississippi, her home town. Her family was poor and struggling, but Earnestine was determined to become a success. I loved to hear her talk with her soft Mississippi accent.

All too quickly, the evening was over. Earnestine and I had spent most of the evening together, dancing and talking. "May I see you again?" I asked her, somewhat hesitantly. I wasn't used to nice girls.

"I'd like that very much," she said.

It was a whirlwind courtship: I took her everywhere. Earnestine was comfortable to be with. She made me feel at ease. I was determined to marry her, and a month after we met, I proposed.

"I love you, Earnestine. Will you marry me?"

"We're too young, Chris," was all she said.

I kept on proposing, nearly every time we were together. Meanwhile, I was having trouble with my parents. They had heard about Earnestine. As far as they were concerned, they had just gotten me out of one scrape and now I was getting into another. First it had looked like I was about to become a gangster, and now—almost as bad in their eyes—I was thinking about marrying a girl who wasn't Greek. They were convinced I was bent on ruining my life.

I kept right on proposing to Earnestine. Finally, she said yes and we got married. My parents were heartbroken. If you weren't Greek, my parents told me, you weren't Greek Orthodox. If you weren't Greek Orthodox, you wouldn't get into heaven. And what about the children? How would they grow up?

Mamma and pappa were sick about my marriage, but I was happy for almost the first time in my life. I had a job I liked and a wife I loved. Earnestine fit in well with the Greek community, learning their ways. She joined the Daughters of Penelope at the Greek Orthodox church and learned to cook Greek-style. We went to the Greek parties together, and Earnestine learned to join in the dances. And she went to the Greek Orthodox church with me faithfully, even though she couldn't understand a word of the Greek service.

Pappa was won over. "That's a fine girl who'll go with her husband," he told me. But mamma was adamant. No non-Greek woman would ever be good enough for her son. For years, mamma and Earnestine had trouble between them as they battled for my affection. My loyalty lay with Earnestine, but my heart was torn. I wanted my two favorite women to love each other.

After I married Earnestine, I lost my urge to be tough. Earnestine was gentle and sweet: she had a calming effect on me. But I had a new ambition, now. I had decided to become a millionaire. I felt sure I could do it, too, but Uncle Steve was constantly putting a damper on all my plans. We fought often.

"You're old-fashioned!" I would yell at him. "You're running this business like it was in the 1930s. Your methods were okay back then, but these are modern times. We're living in the 1950s now!"

"I like it fine," he would say. "This business is just the way I want it. I have all I need. I don't have to take risks. I built this business from a shoeshine stand, and now I have customers all over Texas and Louisiana. If you don't like it, you can leave."

"I think I will," I'd say.

We had that fight so often, we could have made a movie of it, and just run an instant replay each time one of us got mad. Finally, we had it once too often. Instead of letting it blow over as usual, I stewed for days. I had been with Uncle Steve for two years. I had learned all he could teach me. Now I felt like I had learned enough so that I could teach him a thing or two. But he wouldn't listen to any of the suggestions I made.

His old-fashioned business methods infuriated me.

To add to my difficulties, I began to have trouble at home. It started in the middle of the night.

"Chris! Wake up!" Earnestine's voice was trembling as she shook me. "Wake up, Chris!" I'm so scared! I'm so scared!"

I sat up. "What's wrong?" I asked her.

"I had the most frightening dream. I dreamed that Jesus was coming back. And I'm not ready to meet Him!"

Earnestine was shaking and shivering, but I was relieved. For a minute, I'd thought something bad had happened to the baby. Our daughter, Georganna, had arrived just months before. "Tell me about it," I said to her. I was anxious to get back to sleep, but I could see that she was badly frightened.

"I was in a group of people," Earnestine told me, "and we were all outside, watching this little stunt plane. We must have been at an air show. All of a sudden, the sky turned completely black. There were no stars out, or anything. People began to pray and look up. Then the sky began to grow light around the edges and, all of a sudden, I realized that Jesus was coming back to earth.

"I didn't see Him, but I knew He was coming back, and I was not ready to meet Him! I was so afraid. It was the most horrible feeling. I can't put it into words. And I prayed, 'Oh, God, don't let this end! Please let me get a chance to be baptized, and I'll follow You—I'll serve You! Please don't let this be the end!'

"And I heard this voice—I still didn't see anybody—and the voice said, 'Follow Me.' "

I calmed Earnestine as best I could, rolled over, and went back to sleep. But Earnestine couldn't sleep. She sat on the edge of the bed, drenched in sweat. Her heart was pounding. She checked the baby to make sure she was asleep, then went into the living room and asked Jesus to save her, to make her ready for Him when He came back. She could hardly wait until morning, so she could call a minister.

About seven o'clock in the morning, Earnestine couldn't wait any longer. When we were new to the neighborhood, an Episcopal priest had visited us. He was the only minister Earnestine knew to call. She called him and he arranged for her to get baptized and take confirmation.

The next morning, I was sure Earnestine was beside herself. She went to church occasionally, like me, at the Greek Orthodox church. That was enough, wasn't it? I couldn't understand all this fuss over a silly nightmare.

But in the days that followed, Earnestine changed. She read the Bible a lot. And she wanted to go to church. On Sundays, however, I insisted she go to the beach with me in Galveston. Dutifully, she came along. But she really wanted to be in church. Earnestine also went with me to dances and parties when I insisted, but now she didn't enjoy them. I knew she was just coming with me because she thought it would make me happy. I wasn't happy. A man wants his wife to like the same things he does, to participate in his pleasures because she enjoys them too, not just to humor him. Suddenly, I had a rival for Earnestine's affections. But it wasn't a rival I could challenge. How can a man fight God?

God was too big to tackle, so I tackled Steve Panos instead. Soon, we had another fight.

"This boot shop is making thirty thousand dollars a year" I yelled at Uncle Steve. "It ought to be making ninety or a hundred thousand!"

"Now you just listen to me, Mr. Big Shot" he yelled back. "I'm almost seventy years old. I built this business from nothing. I have experience. I know this business. Now you want to come in here, barely twenty years old, only a couple of years' experience, and tell me how to run it. Mr. Instant Big Shot!"

I was so angry, I was afraid to say anything, but I made up my mind to start looking for something else. Thought he knew it all, did he? I'd show him! I didn't need him or the Palace Boot Shop. I would find something else to do. I decided to call my cousin, Johnny Mitchell, and ask him for a job.

My cousins Johnny, George, and Christy Mitchell were all born in Galveston, like me. They had all done well for themselves. George Mitchell was president of Mitchell Energy. Johnny was just beginning a new building and developing venture called Pacesetter Homes. When I called him, he offered me a job selling houses with Norman Dobbins, his partner. Was I interested?

Interested? I was ecstatic! "Would I like to work for you?" I exclaimed. "Would I! Where do I report? When do I start?" I was so excited I could hardly talk. When I hung up the phone, I told Earnestine my dream. "Earnestine, I'm going to be a millionaire before I'm forty. I know I can do it."

I left work at the boot shop. "I'm leaving now," I told Uncle Steve. "But some day, I'll be back to buy you out."

The day after I left the Palace Boot Shop, I reported for work at the model home. Norman showed me the ropes and taught me how to show a house, how to follow up, how to close a sale. His advice was all-inclusive: he told me how to dress, how to act and gave me tips on meeting people. I caught on quickly. Selling houses was easy for me. The customers seemed to take to me right away, and I had learned a lot about selling from Uncle Steve. Six weeks after I started I felt ready to sell the world.

Pacesetter was in the middle of a big promotion, with large ads in all three Houston papers. Our model home was beautifully decorated, and we had houses available for people to move into right away. The economic climate was good, and it was Sunday, a good day to sell houses. Weekdays, most men are at the office; their wives come by and look, but to close the sale the husband has to be there, too.

That Sunday, I sold six houses. It broke a record. None of Norman's salesmen had ever sold that many in one day. "That's fantastic," he told me. "I've never seen anything like it. You've sold more homes today than the rest of my salesmen have sold all week."

I kept on selling. Soon, Norman made me his sales manager. I had my own subdivision. The money was rolling in. I trained new salespeople, and taught them the tricks of the trade that Norman had taught me not long before. I made a percentage of their sales. I tried to infect them with my own enthusiasm.

As I taught the men how to sell, I was also learning all I could from Norman. He showed me how to develop an addition, how to look for land, how to decorate and plan the houses. I watched and learned, dreaming of developing a home-building business of my own one day.

I still planned to become a millionaire.

Chapter Seven
Rags to Riches

Within months of her conversion, my wife had become what I considered to be a religious fanatic. Not knowing quite what to make of the abrupt change in her, I threw myself into my work harder than ever before. Nights, I began to party more, to drink more, to run with a more expensive crowd.

Suddenly, our little house on Hemlock Street seemed small and cramped to me. For one thing, it really was too small for us, now that Georganna had arrived. For another, it didn't quite fit in with the new, high-status image I was carving for myself. It was too unpretentious. Besides, a good salesman has to be sold on the product that he sells, and I was sold on ours. I made a deal with Norman for one of the Pacesetter homes, and we closed right then and there. I could hardly wait to go home and tell Earnestine the news.

As soon as I got home, I dangled the keys in front of Earnestine.

"Do you know what these are for?" I asked.

"No," she answered.

"They're the keys for our new home."

"But Chris," she protested automatically, "we don't have the money now. How can we move to a new home?"

Earnestine's family had been so poor that they'd had to watch every nickel they spent. Lifelong habits are hard to break. Even though I handled the finances and Earnestine had no way of knowing what we could or couldn't afford, she protested anyway. I knew what made her do it, but it irritated me. I had wanted to buy the house and I *had* bought it. It made me so mad I went out and bought a new car to go with the house.

Again, Earnestine started to protest. "It's not that I don't have confidence in you, Chris, but—"

"Listen, darling, that's no way to talk to a man who's going to be a millionaire before he's forty," I interrupted. This time, for some reason, I wasn't upset by her protests. I reassured her and we moved into the new house.

I enjoyed our new house, but I was still dissatisfied. I was making more money than ever before, but I wanted to own my own business, to make some really big money. But I just didn't have the capital I needed. The more dissatisfied I got, the more my mind went back to the Palace Boot Shop and its unused potential. It gave me an idea. I went by to see my Uncle Steve.

Steve's store was just the way I'd left it. Nothing had changed. That was part of the trouble, I thought. Uncle Steve had always been too unwilling to change with the times. I looked at the boot displays and inhaled the familiar odors of polish, leather, and dye.

"I've got a proposition for you," I said to Uncle Steve as soon as I saw him. He looked understandably skeptical.

"Do you remember what I told you when I left?" I asked him. "I told you I'd be back one day to buy you out."

My uncle's expression didn't change. I could practically hear him thinking, "Mr. Instant Big Shot."

"You've got a big mouth. Maybe you better tell me. I'm listening," he said.

I explained the deal I had in mind: I was going to buy him out, and he was going to lend me the money to do it with. He looked like he could hardly believe his ears.

"Let me get this straight. Me loan you the money, so you can buy me out?" he asked. He looked thunderstruck.

It took all the persuasiveness I had and nearly an hour to do it, but I finally convinced him that the deal was good, and that I could make a go of it. Uncle Steve had a quick temper, but underneath his bluff exterior lurked the proverbial heart of gold, and he had faith in my ability. He signed the papers and the Palace Boot Shop was mine.

Immediately, I started to implement the ideas I'd had when I worked for Uncle Steve. First, I expanded the shop to include a line of Western clothing. I changed the name of the shop to Palace Boot and Western Wear and started an extensive advertising campaign. Houston is a big Western wear town, and the response was good. In a short time, our business tripled.

Innovation, publicity, promotion: all were among my strong points. We were the first to make and sell cowboy boots with metallic trim, and we got good newspaper coverage when I presented a pair of the new metallic trim boots to Johnny Crawford, star of the TV show, *The Rifleman*. We got still more publicity when I presented boots to the Queen of the Houston Fat Stock Show in 1960. I also made boots for various other celebrities: Maxine Messenger, the society columnist for the *Houston Chronicle*, Sonny Look, whose family owned the Sir Loin steakhouses, and Bubba Becker of the jewelry family.

I began to party more, to drink more. Sonny Look and

Bubba Becker became friends of mine, and I also ran around with the rodeo crowd. Earnestine and I went to all the biggest social events of the city. I was made a deputy sheriff, joined the Chamber of Commerce, and took a prominent part in the Houston Fat Stock Show. Soon the gossip columns of the *Houston Post* and the *Houston Chronicle* began to feature my name and picture more and more.

I began staying out all night playing poker or partying at the Elks and other clubs where there would be dancing and drinking. I had many friends among the club set and used to drink with Glenn McCarthy, who built and owned what was then the Shamrock Hotel and is now the Shamrock Hilton. Financially and socially, I was a success. Inside, I was empty.

During those days, about the only time I spent with my family was on Sundays, when we went to the beach at Galveston. I would take beer or whiskey along, and pass the time with that. Earnestine wouldn't join me. She had never enjoyed drinking, and the more she saw me drink, the less she wanted to acquire a taste for it. But even though I was moderately under the influence on those occasions, Earnestine always seemed to enjoy my company.

On the business front, things were going well. We had started an investment banking and mortgage loan firm. I was developing and building homes. I was making money hand over fist, but somewhere along the line, the edge had worn off. When I hadn't had much money, I wanted to be a millionaire, but now that I had plenty of money, the dream had dimmed. I had all the money that I really needed. I still planned on becoming a millionaire, but it wasn't the burning desire that it had been. Success seemed certain, but I sensed that it wasn't going to fill the emptiness I felt. Somehow, it seemed like I was back to being the Greek again. I was living the same kind of life, but in a higher tax bracket. I began to get restless. One morning, I phoned Uncle Steve.

"Steve, I have lost interest in the boot shop. I would like for you to take it back over again." He agreed and I got out of the boot business. It left me free to concentrate on the more lucrative businesses I now had going. But the businesses were disappointing. I was still restless, still searching.

I continued striving for enjoyment, hoping to find satisfaction in my wild night life. The more I drank and stayed out late, the closer Earnestine got to God. The closer Earnestine got to God, the more I drank and stayed out late. It seemed like a vicious circle. In my own drunken way, I was fighting her religion tooth and nail. Earnestine sought comfort during this time by reading the Bible for hours on end, by praying late into the night, and by going to services at the Episcopal church. She meant to try anything that might help, and she knew we needed a miracle. She could see that our lives were falling apart, but I wouldn't admit it to myself. On occasion, however, I began to toy with the idea of suicide.

One morning, Earnestine was attending an Altar Guild meeting, but she couldn't seem to concentrate on what was going on. Some of her friends had invited her to a house-prayer meeting and her mind was full of fearful doubts and questions about whether to attend or not.

As the meeting progressed, the presiding officer called on the main speaker, a woman from a church across town.

"I want the Lord to have all the glory," the speaker said, "so I won't speak from the front. I want you all to look at the cross. Think about Jesus; don't think about me. I don't want you to look at me. Instead, I want to tell you about God, and about what He has done for me—"

At the front of the church there was a table covered with a white linen cloth. On the table was a large gold cross. As she looked at the table, Earnestine began to see something glowing on the snowy fabric. At first, it looked like a splash of light. Then slowly, very slowly, a face appeared. It was the face of Jesus, glowing on the surface of the cloth.

The more Earnestine looked at the face, the more upset she got. "There must be a picture under the cloth," she thought, "with a light behind it. But I'm on the Altar Guild! I helped them set that table up. I know there is no picture there!"

She became more and more upset. The face of Jesus glowed there on the cloth, inscrutable. Earnestine prayed, "Lord, what are You trying to tell me? Do You want me to go to that meeting? Lord, what do You want? What do You want me to do?" The Lord gave no audible answer.

As soon as the meeting was over, Earnestine hurried to find her friend Madge. Without preamble, she rushed up and asked, "Is there a picture of Jesus under the altar cloth?"

"No," Madge answered. "Why do you ask?"

"Did you see a picture of Jesus on the altar cloth during the talk?"

"No," Madge said. "All I saw was the cloth and the cross. What's wrong?"

Earnestine began to cry.

As she cried, Father Newman walked up to Madge and Earnestine. Madge explained, "She's seen a vision of Jesus on the altar cloth." Father Newman comforted Earnestine so kindly that she began to feel differently about the church, about the prayer group. If Father Newman could be so understanding, she thought, maybe these people weren't that bad. And maybe that was what Jesus had been trying to tell her. Earnestine decided to attend. It might not be so awful after all.

Chapter Eight
End of the Road

Tracts. Bibles. Books on God. I found them all over the house, and even in the car. It upset me. I was sure Earnestine was planting them where I would find them. She denied it, but I knew. She was out to get me, to draw me into this crazy religion kick of hers. You never knew what you'd be finding next.

What I found next was a prayer meeting.

I had parked my car and let myself in by the back door. I heard a man speaking. I peeked inside. It looked like every chair in the house had been corralled in our den, and every one of them was occupied. Earnestine's prayer group had invaded my house. Today, of all days. This was the last day I wanted to run into that fanatical group of hers.

It had already been a bad day for me. I had had a few too many at lunch, and had gone to Steve's boot shop somewhat under the influence. When I got there, one of Steve's men had said something to me that just wasn't funny. I took a swing at him. He ducked. My fist whizzed past his head and through Steve's plate glass window. As I was pulling it out, a sharp shard of glass had gashed my forearm. The whole incident had been stupid. I was drunk, disgusted, angry, and in pain. And now this.

"Those blasted fanatics," I thought. "They go to church on Sunday. Then they have to do this religion stuff all week. Isn't once a week enough? They talk about Jesus Christ like He was some kind of friend of theirs, not God Almighty. They're way out in left field. This is just too much."

Disgusted, I eavesdropped on the meeting. The man was saying, "You know Jess, the man we prayed for last week? Well, he died yesterday. The Lord took him home."

"Dear God," a woman's voice prayed. "We love you, we adore you, we praise your holy name. We thank you for Jess and for allowing us to know him for a little while. We thank you that we were able to pray with him and for him. We thank you that you have taken him home to be with you."

The prayer about Jess went on interminably. All that fuss about praying for Jess. And Jess had died! What good had their prayers done him? And these people weren't even upset. They acted like something good had happened to him, he had "gone home to be with Jesus," and they were *happy* about it. I couldn't understand it. I was angry and my arm hurt.

When the prayer ended, I went over to the doorway. Earnestine spotted the bandage on my arm immediately. "What happened to you?" she asked anxiously.

I didn't want to go into it. "I had a little accident," I told her. It *was* an accident, I thought. After all, I had been planning to hit the man, not the window.

Father Scovell came over and joined us. "What have you done to your arm?" he asked me.

"Nothing. Had a little accident, that's all." I was sure he didn't believe me.

"That's too bad. It must hurt. Let me pray for you, Mr. Panos," the priest replied.

I drew back. I didn't like the results of their prayers, if Jess was any indication. I didn't want them praying for me. "No thank you," I said.

The prayer group joined in, all asking to pray for my arm.

"I heard you talking about Jess," I told the room at large. "You prayed for that guy and he's dead. That kind of prayer I don't need. I'm Greek Orthodox. I have everything I need in the Greek Orthodox church. I don't need any help from you, thanks." I made my tone of voice as nasty as possible. "Besides," I added, "my grandfather was a Greek Orthodox priest." If they wanted to play religion, I could play religion too. How many of them had clergy in the family?

Father Scovell didn't reply to any of this tirade. Instead, he looked at me calmly and said, "Just remember, Chris, Jesus loves you."

I headed for my well-stocked bar and found a jug of *retsina*, the strong, resin-flavored wine of Greece. It has a bouquet faintly reminiscent of turpentine, and most Americans who drink it for the first time don't like it. I waved the jug at the priest.

"I'll let you pray for me if you'll have a drink with me," I told him. Struck with the idea, I repeated the offer to the group at large. Everyone refused, except the priest. He seemed to know that it was a test of whether I would participate or not. But I found some excuse to keep them from praying for me anyway. I didn't want to end up like Jess. I was tired of living, yes. But I was also afraid to die.

From then on, I avoided the prayer group as much as possible, although I grew to like Father Scovell. I would enter the house just as I knew the prayer group would be breaking up, and chat with the priest. In spite of myself, I liked him. No matter how rudely I spoke to him, he always responded as though I was a friend of his.

One afternoon, I came home early. There was no sense in going back to work: I was drunk. I had had a long, late lunch. I'd drunk more than I'd eaten and could hardly walk straight.

"I want to die," I told Earnestine when I stumbled in. I sat at our kitchen table, so drunk I could hardly sit up. I'm going to get my gun, or run my car off a cliff, or take poison. Life isn't worth it."

Frightened, Earnestine ran to the telephone and dialed. I listened in. If she was calling the cops or something, I was getting out of there. It wasn't the cops.

"Father Scovell," I heard her whisper, "please come over right away. I need help."

Father Scovell, I thought, would be harmless. I continued to ramble about suicide.

Father Scovell appeared in no time. "Hello, Chris," he began. The sight of his black suit and clerical collar filled me with anger.

"What are you doing here?" I demanded. Drunks have short memories.

"I am here to talk about your relationship to God," he told me. He was unruffled by my anger. "I understand you are thinking of killing yourself."

"What I'm thinking of doing is none of your business," I told him. "My life is my business and nobody else's."

"It's my business too, Chris," the priest told me. "It's my business because I love you and God loves you."

"I don't need any of that," I told him angrily, grabbing the front of his shirt, just below the hated clerical collar. Pulling Father Scovell's face close to mine, I roared, "I have all the help I need. Leave me alone, just leave me alone. I don't need anything from you. Get out of here! If I see you again, I'll hit you in the mouth!"

Father Scovell calmly took my hand from the front of his shirt. He smoothed down the wrinkles I'd made and looked at me.

"I'll go, Chris," he told me. "But remember—I love you. The answer to the problems of your life is Jesus Christ."

Earnestine had watched the whole encounter. She was ashamed of me, embarrassed by my behavior, and tired of living with a drunken, hostile man who either stayed out late at night or came home early only to insult her friends. She made up her mind to leave me.

At the next meeting of the prayer group, she shared her decision.

"I can't go on like this any longer," Earnestine told the group. "Chris has changed so much. He's drunk so often. He stays out all night sometimes. He insults my friends. It's not good for the children to grow up with an alcoholic daddy. What if they grow up to be like him? I can't take any more of it. I'm going to leave."

The prayer group rose to my defense. "We know things are bad," Father Scovell told her. "But what did you expect? When you started praying for him, did you think things would get better immediately? God answers prayer, but He doesn't always work the way we want Him to.

"Right now, Chris can't help the way he's acting. Now, he's serving the devil. When he gets saved, he will serve God. In the meantime, try to look on his drinking as a sickness. You wouldn't leave him if he were sick, would you? Put him on the altar and leave him there. Give God time to work."

So Earnestine decided to stay with me. But it wasn't easy. Most of all, she hated to see the man she had married become a drunken bum right before her eyes. Finally, one night she felt she just couldn't take any more.

"Lord," she prayed, "I just can't stand this. You know he's making money, he's supporting me well, but his drinking is getting worse and worse. I won't leave him, Lord, since I promised to live with him for better or for worse. But Lord, if it isn't going to get better, if he isn't going to change, then take him. Please change him or take him."

God nearly took me.

Chapter Nine
SMASH-UP!

The angrier I got, the faster I drove.

Sam, my building foreman, sat in the seat beside me, his right foot reaching often for an imaginary brake pedal. His lips were pressed together, and his body was tense. When I'd lurch around a corner, he would grab for the arm rest on the door.

It was raining, and the street lights washed streaks of gold across the blacktop. Christmas lights twinkled. The lights were beautiful against the wet black night, but I was too angry and too drunk to notice. I had lost a lot at poker, and the other players had been razzing me. I was tired of it.

"Come on, Sam," I'd said. "Let's get out of here." We'd gone to my car.

"Chris," Sam had told me, "you've had a lot to drink. Maybe I'd better drive."

I had laughed at him. All that fuss about a little booze! I'd been drinking since I was a kid. I could hold my liquor. I was able to drive.

I fumbled with the car keys as I unlocked the doors of my car. We drove off. The windshield wipers slapped the rain away, keeping time to my thoughts as I drove towards Sam's house to drop him off. Earnestine would be surprised to see me so early. It was only one o'clock. Usually I didn't come home from a poker game until much later. I stepped on the accelerator.

"Chris," Sam yelled. "Slow down! You're going too fast. You'll kill us!"

I laughed and pressed my foot down even harder. The heavy car zoomed forward, toward South Post Oak Road. As I turned onto South Post Oak, going much too fast, the car skidded on the rain-slicked pavement. Sam grabbed for the hand rest, his face white.

"You're chicken, Sam," I taunted him.

South Post Oak Road stretched up ahead of us, gleaming wetly. Too late, I saw a sharp bend in the road. I swung the wheel sharply but the car screeched off the road and hurtled towards a tree. The last thing I remember is seeing a tree coming at me through the windshield, and feeling a terrible pain in my face.

The car uprooted the tree and settled into the bayou at the side of the road. Miraculously, Sam wasn't hurt. He pulled himself out of the mud and got over to me. My face was a mess. It was cut in several places, and one eye was hanging out of its socket. One side of my face was all smashed in.

"My God," Sam thought. "My God, he's dead. I knew we'd have a wreck, and now he's dead." He put his hand on my chest and he felt a heartbeat. He pulled and tugged at my inert body and dragged me out of the window of the wreck. He struggled to get me up the bank and onto the shoulder of the road. There was no traffic. Sam looked frantically up and down the silent road.

After what seemed an eternity, Sam saw a pair of headlights coming toward us. Sam stood in the center of the road and flagged the car down. Together, Sam and the driver got me into the car and on the back seat. I was still unconscious when they arrived at Bellaire Hospital.

A policeman asked Sam, "How did it happen?"

"He was driving too fast and lost control. Is he going to die?"

"Looks like he might. Is he married?"

"Yes, he is," Sam told the policeman. He gave the policeman Earnestine's phone number. The policeman called her, told her what had happened and said that she was needed at the Bellaire Hospital to sign a release for surgery. She said she would come.

Hanging up the phone, Earnestine began to pray as she got ready. "Lord, save his soul. I meant what I said when I asked you to save him or take him, but if it's your will to take him, please save his soul before you do. Please, please don't let him die unsaved."

When Earnestine got to the hospital, she found that the doctors were afraid to operate right away because I was so drunk, and in deep shock. They made me as comfortable as they could, staunched the flow of blood, and waited.

So far as the doctors could tell, I was unconscious. But my mind had continued to function. I knew I was drunk and weak from loss of blood. I didn't know whether I would live or die. As I lay there, it was as if my whole life passed in review before me. I watched fights I had had as a little boy. I watched myself stealing money from the cash register and disobeying my parents. I saw myself drunkenly trying to kill the tarantulas in the park, fighting with the Mexican, meeting Earnestine. I saw myself working in the boot shop, building a business empire, drinking and dancing, neglecting my wife and children. I saw it all.

As I watched, it was as though I saw my life on a giant

71

balance sheet. The plusses were added up on one side; the minuses were subtracted on the other. As I watched, I saw that my life totaled up to a great big zero. Then a puff of smoke appeared. The smoke was gray and black, and a dark, sinister figure emerged from its center. It was the devil. He grinned terribly.

"Chris Panos," he said, "I have saved you from death. Now you will be a millionaire. The thing you greatly desired has come to pass. All you have to do is bow down your heart to me."

I shrank back. I was terrified. The devil watched me, waiting, waiting—

Suddenly a blinding light filled the room and the darkness vanished. Out of the center of the light stepped the same man I had seen in the park when I was a child. It was Jesus Christ. He reached out and laid His hand on mine. He said, "Chris Panos, I saved you for a purpose. You are to preach My Bible in all the world." The Lord spoke to me in Greek, the language of my childhood. Instantly, a supernatural life and peace flowed into me. I felt as though my whole body was being lifted into the air. Deep inside of me, I felt a change take place. I had been born again.

Jesus stayed with me that night, speaking again. The words He spoke are familiar to those who read their Bibles, but they were not familiar to me. He told me, "Chris, I am the Way, the Truth, and the Life. No man comes to the Father except by Me." His words eased me, calmed me.

Soon, the surgeons decided that it would be safe to operate. It was around three o'clock in the morning when I was wheeled into the operating room. The doctors had a lot to do. There was internal bleeding. The bones around my eye were crushed. My nose was broken, and my sinuses were pierced. My jaw was broken in four places. They did as much as they could safely accomplish, stopping the flow of blood and rebuilding the bones around my eye with wire and plastic. They worked for hours. Finally they decided not to prolong the operation any longer. My system had taken all that it could take. They postponed setting the bones in my jaw until another time.

Chapter Ten
Don't Monkey Around

When I came to in the hospital, I had needles in my arm and tubes in my nose. My face was bandaged, and I was in pain. And there was Earnestine along with every member of her Thursday prayer group. Standing around my bed were the people who had prayed for me for over two years, the people I had hated. Suddenly, surprisingly, I found I didn't hate them any longer. I loved them. I felt joy, peace, contentment. I closed my eyes and drifted off to sleep.

Later, Earnestine told me that when I had come out of the operating room, I had been in a delirium of pain. Even though I was heavily sedated, the agony had been so intense that it took both Earnestine and a full-time nurse to keep me from pulling the bandages off my face. After about a half an hour of this awful struggle, Earnestine took time out to call Father Newman and the members of the prayer group, who immediately rushed to the hospital. After they prayed, I quieted down and went to sleep.

I spent most of my time that week drifting in and out of

sleep. I was drugged, and nurses kept arriving with various shots and pills to kill infection and subdue the pain. In my moments of awareness, I returned over and over again to the vision I had received, treasuring it in my heart, storing the details in my spirit. My jaws were immobilized, but even if they hadn't been, I couldn't have told Earnestine about it. Not yet. To me, it was too precious a thing to share.

It was a week before the doctors considered me well enough to attempt to set my broken jawbones, and meanwhile they kept me heavily sedated. The drugs began to worry Earnestine. She knew all too well what it was like living with a heavy drinker; she didn't want to have to go through life living with a drug addict as well. One afternoon, I overheard her talking to the doctor in the hall outside my door.

"Doctor, I'm worried about all these shots," she told him. "They're giving Chris so much dope. Do you have to give him so many narcotics?"

"If we didn't give him the pain killers, Mrs. Panos, he wouldn't be able to stand the pain," the doctor told her. "We are doing all we can. We will try to set those bones in his jaws soon, and after that we will scale down the dosage as soon as possible."

"Do you have any idea when he'll be well enough to come home?" Earnestine asked him next.

"No, Mrs. Panos, I'm sorry but I don't. It's much too soon to tell. It might be two months, it might be three months. He was smashed up pretty badly, and these things don't mend overnight, you know."

Lying in my bed and listening to the doctor, I felt calm and at peace. I wasn't worried. I knew I would be going home soon—sooner than the doctor thought. Jesus would take care of it.

Jesus wasn't just taking care of my physical and spiritual

well being, He was taking care of my business affairs as well. Many of my friends in the building business came to visit me, like Lester Prokop of Prokop Building and Lumber Company, along with many other prominent Houston builders. "Don't worry about the business," they reassured me. "Don't even think about it. Just get well. We'll look after everything till you're back on your feet."

Full of newborn faith in God, I began to pray that I'd be home in time for Christmas. The accident had happened on December 8. On December 21, I was released from the hospital. It was the miracle I'd prayed for, and I couldn't have received a better Christmas present from the Lord.

Just before I was to leave for home, the doctor came by to talk to Earnestine and me. "I have something very important to tell you before I let you out of here," he said to me. "As you know, your jaws are wired shut. Those bones were broken in four places, and we are going to have to keep them immobilized for several months. You can drink malts and soups, like we've been feeding you here in the hospital. You can drink anything Mrs. Panos can whip up in the blender. But there's one thing that you can't drink." He paused, emphasizing the importance of his next statement. "Under *no* circumstances are you to take any alcohol. And I am not just moralizing. I am not trying to get you to give it up for life. But I want you to understand that right now this is a matter of life and death importance. If you take even one drink, it might react with the painkillers you're taking and make you drunk. If you get drunk, you might vomit. If you vomit, with your jaws wired together like that, you will strangle on your own vomit."

The doctor looked at Earnestine. Earnestine looked at me. They both looked very worried. She knew how headstrong I had always been. If I wanted to take a drink, Earnestine didn't see how she could stop me. She knew nothing about my conversion; any changes that she had noted, she'd attributed to the accident and the drugs.

Since the accident, however, I had discovered new changes in myself with every passing day. When Jesus had appeared to me, He had cleansed me inside. Old habits dropped off. New habits began to form. Though I had drunk heavily since my early teens, I found I did not even want to drink now.

Having my jaws wired together was very inconvenient. I couldn't eat the foods I liked, and I could barely talk, because I had to say everything with my teeth clamped together. But inconvenient as it was, I still didn't want to curse the way I would have done before the accident. Instead, over and over again I found myself humming the paschal anthem, *Christos Anesti*—Christ Is Risen.

Earnestine bustled around the house, making me comfortable and preparing for Christmas. She had to make her preparations quickly. She had not felt like doing anything for Christmas when she had thought that I would be in the hospital, but now that I was home, she wanted to celebrate.

Earnestine was happy during that time, even though she didn't realize that her prayers for me had already been answered beyond her wildest dreams. Just having me at home as an invalid was better than things had been before. She knew where I was and what I was doing. Georganna and Chrissy were happy their daddy was home.

Hampered by the hardware in my mouth, I continued to hum *Christos Anesti*. I wanted to shout it, I was so full of joy, but humming would do. I read my Bible and watched a lot of television. One show that sticks in my mind was a movie entitled *The Keys of the Kingdom*. It starred Gregory Peck who portrayed a Roman Catholic missionary to China. I was strangely moved. I remembered the vision: "I have called you to preach My Bible to all the world." The Lord seemed to be asking me, "Chris Panos, would you go to the ends of the earth for Me?" I pondered the question, turning it over in my mind and spirit. The answer was an unqualified yes.

Mamma noticed the change in me before Earnestine did. She was worried sick and so was pappa. They came over often, watching me carefully. Finally, she could stand the suspense no longer.

"What has happened to you, son?" mamma asked, speaking in Greek so Earnestine couldn't understand. "What has happened to you? You're acting so strangely."

"Nothing, mamma," I answered, through my clenched teeth.

"Maybe when you were thrown in the bayou, it twisted your mind. Maybe you've gone crazy."

"No, mamma. I haven't twisted my mind. I've just seen Jesus."

"Oh no!" mamma cried. "You've got another religion. Earnestine has led you off in that strange religion of hers."

"No, mamma," I told her. "I have no new religion. I have just seen Jesus."

"Are you still a good Greek Orthodox?"

"Yes, mamma. I have just seen Jesus."

I told her then about my vision, although I didn't tell her everything. I didn't tell her I had been called to preach. Mamma thought back over the incident in the park at Fort Worth. This was the second time that I had claimed to see the Lord. Maybe I had, she thought. After all, she had seen Him. So why shouldn't I see Him?

When I saw the Lord as a boy, mamma had seen no change in me. Now she had seen a change. She saw a new son, one who read the Bible and did not argue with her.

Pappa had listened quietly to the exchange between me and mamma. "I don't know what he has," he told mamma. "But whatever it is, I want it too." Kneeling on the rug in our home, my sweet pappa accepted Jesus as his own personal Savior not too long after I was released from the hospital. I had my first convert.

The first Thursday evening in 1962, I told Earnestine that I wanted to go to the prayer group with her. She was pleased, but she thought it was just because I had nothing better to do.

To Earnestine's delight, I began attending the Thursday prayer meetings—both morning and evening—regularly. Before, I had had an intense desire to stay away from anything having to do with Earnestine's religion. Now, I began to go to church with her.

It took quite a while for her to discover that I had become a Christian. What threw her off, I think, is that I didn't talk like the Christians she knew. They punctuated their sentences with expressions like "Praise the Lord," "Hallelujah," and "Amen!" But I maintained the same vocabulary that I had always had, minus the curses.

As soon as the wires were out of my jaws, I returned to work. John Swenson, my partner, noticed the change in me immediately.

"What's happened to you, Chris? Before the accident, you used to swear a blue streak. Now all you do is smile and read your Bible."

"I've become a Christian, John," I told him.

John, a Christian himself, was happy to learn that I had found the Lord. Earnestine and I began to spend a lot of time socializing with the Swensons. We had planned to have dinner at their house one night, when I was approached by our new lady sales manager about a real estate deal. She was a real whiz at her job. That evening she asked me to drop by her house on my way home "to talk about a land deal." When I arrived, she offered me a drink, and not thinking, I accepted. I had just reached out to take it when there was a loud crash outside. "What's that?" she asked.

I put down the drink untasted and opened the door. Someone had bashed in the side of my new car and driven off. Filled with sudden fear, I jumped in my car and drove away, not even bidding the sales manager goodbye. I realized what I had been about to do. I had been standing in that woman's living room about to take a drink. The wires were out of my jaws by now, so I would not have been in any physical danger. But it was not physical danger that concerned me. My danger had been spiritual.

"Oh, Lord, what I was about to do!" I prayed in anguish as I drove. "Lord, what I almost did! I could have gotten myself into all kinds of trouble!" I was so frightened, my heart was pounding.

As I rushed home, a Voice spoke in my ear. "Chris Panos," He said, "Don't monkey around with Me!"

"Yes, Lord," I breathed.

Halfway home, I remembered that I was supposed to meet Earnestine at the Swensons'. I drove there and told them my experience. We all had a good laugh, and then John Swenson quietly explained the incident to me.

"Chris, the Bible tells us very plainly that we must not tempt the Lord our God. It means exactly what it says. We must not tempt God. You probably could have taken that drink. You probably could have been there alone with her, but it was a temptation. You were doing something that you shouldn't do."

I was so relieved to have been saved from doing what I might have done, that I didn't even mind paying the bill to have my car repaired. God hadn't spoken eloquently to me. He had spoken plainly in a language that I could understand. From now on, I resolved, I would be more careful. I knew that I would have to stay on guard, watching to see that none of my old bad habits reasserted themselves. Because I knew now that I must not play around with God.

Chapter Eleven
A Little Bit of Heaven

My heart was thumping and my hands were perspiring as I got ready to board the plane from Houston to California. I had flown only short hops before, but never any distance. I don't know why it was that flying, of all things, should make me nervous. But it did. Always before, I'd gotten my courage for these airborne ventures from a bottle, but this time I was boarding the plane cold sober. For a minute I wondered how I'd gotten myself committed to this trip. Imagine voluntarily getting into an airplane, so soon after nearly being killed in a car. I ought to have my head examined.

Actually, of course, my head had been examined quite a bit in the recent past, as the doctors checked their reconstruction work. I'd gone back to work as soon as the wires were out of my jaws, about a month after they'd let me out of the hospital. In addition to my business activities, I'd also started to attend Earnestine's prayer group, and the Episcopal church with her on Sundays. There, I astounded the congregation by carrying my Bible with me. It was something the Episcopalians didn't do. I became known as "the man who carries his Bible."

A few days before I boarded the plane, however, I had received a call from Father Scovell. That call was to have tremendous influence on my life.

"Chris," Father Scovell had told me, "I'm in Van Nuys, California. I flew down a few days ago from Canada to visit my friends George and Virginia Otis. There are some people here I think the Lord wants you to meet. I'd like you to fly on out."

We had talked for a while, and I had agreed to fly out a few days later.

We had heard from Father Scovell occasionally after he moved to Canada, but I had not expected an invitation like this. Still, if he said he thought it would be good for me to meet these people, I knew I'd better take him up on the offer. I was hungry for spiritual growth, and ready to fly, if need be, to find it.

"I'm awfully nervous," I told Earnestine, who had accompanied me to the airport. "You know how nervous flying makes me."

"God has arranged this meeting," she told me. "He will keep you safe."

She had more faith than I had. I was still nervous when I got on the plane, but sometime during that three-hour flight I forgot about my nervousness. The flight went smoothly. I read the Bible and hummed a little tune the Lord had given me.

I made the short hop from the airport in L.A. to George Otis's home in Van Nuys by helicopter. As a builder, I was impressed by his large, luxurious chalet-style house. But I was even more impressed by the people I met, George and Virginia Otis, Rita Reed, who was later to become the wife of Dennis Bennett, and Harald Bredesen.

For three solid weeks we had a glorious time. We would sit around the swimming pool and praise the Lord, then we'd talk a little business, then we'd talk about our ministries, then praise the Lord again. It was a blessed time in the Lord, a little bit of heaven.

God was just beginning to use George Otis to testify to movie stars. During the time I was there, he must have spoken to over a hundred guests, many of them famous, telling them about his newfound relationship with God. Seeing him witnessing to these celebrities confirmed something in my own spirit. God had been telling me that He would use me to bring the gospel to many world leaders. I hadn't seen how I could do such a thing, but now God was providing me with an object lesson.

As we sat around the swimming pool or gathered in the Otis's sunken living room, we also talked about Bible Voice, then in its planning stages. At that time, the company had nothing to do with publishing: it was being set up to spread the gospel in record form. They planned to record the Bible with Dennis Bennett doing the reading.

Derek Prince and Harald Bredesen were also involved in Bible Voice, but Derek Prince was in town mainly because of a teaching seminar being held by the Blessed Trinity Society.

Bobby Ewing, who had helped start New Testament churches in Waco, Texas and throughout the United States, also dropped by the Otis home. God had given Bobby Ewing a word for me. "There's a man you need to meet back in Texas," he told me. "His name is Jack Locker. I believe God wants you to have a close friendship."

In addition to the more spiritual things that were going on, we did talk a little business. The more I told George Otis about Modern Trend Homes, the more George decided that homebuilding was a good field to be in. Finally, we decided that George really should become my partner. Quickly, we concluded the business part of the deal.

All too soon, it was time to get back to Houston. In three short weeks I had grown enormously in the Lord. I had met men who would become giants in the work of God. And I had a brand-new business partner. But as I flew back to Houston, the man I thought about was a man whom I had never met: Jack Locker, the man from Texas whom I had traveled to California to learn about.

I didn't have long to wait before meeting him. He was scheduled to speak in Houston shortly after I returned from California. I was looking forward to meeting this man I had heard so much about.

The night of the meeting, Earnestine and I went to hear Jack minister. When I saw him, I was stunned. I was used to dressing in the height of fashion; Jack looked like he didn't know what fashion was. He was dressed in an old blue suit and a little, narrow, out-of-style tie. Even his shoes looked years out of date. And Jack himself was a perfectly ordinary looking man about forty years of age. I don't know what I had expected a man of God to look like, but I hadn't expected him to look like Jack.

I was surprised by his appearance, but I knew God intended to use him to teach me many things. As he preached, I prayed silently in my spirit. I knew that God had called me to preach the gospel to all the world, but I also knew that I was unprepared to do so. I needed teaching and training. I knew that God had appointed Jack to provide some of the preparation that I needed.

When the service was over, I went up to talk with him. He was expecting me.

"If you are interested in the word of God I will do everything I can to help you," Jack told me. "If you are not interested, I don't have time to mess with you."

Later on, he set up a regular program of Bible reading for me. "Chris, I want you to follow this plan every day. Each morning when you get up, read two chapters of the Old Testament, two chapters of the New Testament, five Psalms, and one chapter of Proverbs. That way, you will read through the Old Testament every year, the New Testament every four months, and the Books of Psalms and Proverbs monthly.

"You can read more, of course, but don't read less. You have to let the word of God dwell in you richly. It must be there in your spirit, so that the Holy Spirit can call it to your remembrance when you need it. The word of God has to become a living part of you. You must read it, quote it, eat it, sleep it, breathe it, and let it be your very life.

Thus began a God-ordained apprenticeship. Jack taught me often. Although he lived in Waco, he would drive frequently to Houston to spend a day, an afternoon, or even an hour with me. Between his visits, I saturated myself with Bible reading.

I started Jack's plan immediately, and I have followed it faithfully ever since. I read, prayed, and meditated. Often, I would get up at three in the morning to read and pray before going to my office.

Soon, Jack started to take me with him to his speaking engagements. We traveled across Texas into Louisiana, New Mexico, Oklahoma. As we traveled, Jack continued to teach me.

"Sometimes, Chris, God will put a word in your mind. He will want you to see what it means. If you get a word in your mind like that, you should find out what God is saying. Get a good concordance and look the word up. Study the Scripture reference. Find out what God is trying to tell you. Don't take anything He says lightly. The key to growth is consecration. You must be consecrated—sincere, serious, dedicated to following Christ. The Bible says God is a rewarder of them that diligently seek Him. Be diligent in seeking God."

As Jack and I traveled the Southwest, I realized that God was putting me through a time of preparation. Moses spent forty years in Pharoah's court and another forty years tending sheep before he began his ministry. Before God used Paul, God sent him into Arabia for a season of preparation. Before God started to use me, He sent me across the Southwest with Jack.

My ministry began in small ways. As we traveled, Jack encouraged me to give my testimony. Each time I gave it, it became easier to give. Jack introduced me to men of God and encouraged me to read about the spiritual giants of the past.

Several years passed. I read the works of E.W. Kenyon, T.L. Osborn, Bosworth, Charles Price, and others. I was in Billy Graham's and Morris Cerullo's crusades. Gradually, I branched out on my own. I began to get invitations to speak at Full Gospel Business Men's meetings, telling others about how the Lord had saved me. But I didn't mention my call to preach to anyone. It was too personal a thing, something between me and God.

Eventually a big Lutheran church in Minneapolis invited me to bring a sermon. I accepted the invitation, but it worried me. I was used to giving my testimony, but preaching was something else again. Finally, I had it out with the Lord.

"Lord," I prayed, "you've got to help me. Anyone can get up there in the pulpit and talk till their time is up. But I don't want to do that. When I preach, Lord, I want those people to know that you are real. Lord, I need power."

"You don't need to worry about power," the Lord seemed

to impress upon me. "Just preach the gospel. My word has the power to do its own work."

"Well," I told myself, "maybe I'm not sure what preaching the gospel is yet. But God told me that His word had the power to do its own work. Therefore, if a message brings salvation, miracles, and healing when someone else preaches it, it ought to bring salvation, miracles, and healing when *I* preach it, because God's word is in it. If T.L. Osborn's sermons work for T.L. Osborn, why, they ought to work for me!"

The Lord didn't say anything, but I had peace about it. I memorized a sermon of T.L. Osborn's for the date in Minneapolis. When the time came, I stood in the pulpit with sweating palms. My breath came rapidly. I was nervous and confident at the same time. I was uncertain of my own abilities, but I was sure that God would honor His word.

I opened my Bible on the pulpit and started to preach T.L. Osborn's sermon word for word. The power of God settled over the congregation. When I was nearly through with the sermon, I felt impressed to stop. God had told me about a healing.

"There is a woman here tonight with multiple sclerosis," I said. I looked out over the congregation and pointed my finger at a woman sitting in the back row. "God has healed you tonight."

Immediately, she tried to stand. For a minute, it looked like she was going to fall, and two men reached out to steady her, grabbing her arms.

"Let go of her," I said. "In the name of Jesus," I told her, "I command you to walk!"

Shaking off the men's hands, the woman started up the aisle towards the pulpit, going faster and faster. By the time she was halfway up the aisle she was running. Several others were healed that night, but more importantly, many were saved. We gave an altar call at the end of the service, and the front of the church was full of people who had come forward to seek the Lord.

Borrowed sermon or not, God had honored His word.

Chapter Twelve
The Making of a Spy

More and more often, I got invitations to preach. And more and more often, God gave me messages of my own. They brought the same results as the one I'd memorized of Osborn's, but I felt more comfortable with mine. They had, after all, been tailor-made for me.

Besides showing me how to preach the gospel, God had other lessons for me to learn.

One day I was preaching at Lakewood Church in Houston when God drew my attention to a woman seated in a wheelchair. "Go to that lady," God commanded, "and pull her out of the chair."

I grabbed the woman's hand. "Get up," I said.

"No," she answered, pulling back.

"Get up," I insisted. "Walk in the name of Jesus!"

She refused to budge.

"Pull her out of her chair," the Lord said, repeating His original instructions. You have to be *very* sure you've heard

God's voice, before you do a thing like that. I was sure. I pulled.

The woman stood there, wobbling uncertainly. She reached down for the arm of the wheelchair, but I pushed her hand away so that she had to stand unaided. As if to steady herself, she took a step. And another step. And another. Soon she was running. She ran all over the building that night.

Three days later, I got a call from the friend who had brought her to the meeting.

"She's back in the wheelchair again," he reported. He sounded close to tears. "She sat back down in it again last night and now she can't get up again. She was just fine until then, but now—"

I didn't know what to say. I sought the Lord as soon as I hung up.

"Father," I asked, "what happened? That woman was healed. Now she can't get out of her chair. What went wrong?"

"She was healed by the word of faith in your heart," God said. "Later she began to fear and doubt. Next time, you must place the word of faith in *her* heart. Preach the word and God's faith will make her whole."

After that, I began to preach more on faith. But now I saw that it was not enough for me to have faith when people came for prayer. They had to have faith too. Unless the word of God was planted in their hearts, the devil could rob them of their healing.

As the months passed, God gave me more and more opportunities to preach. One morning, as I was praying before going to the office, God spoke to me.

"I have given you the land," He said. I wondered what He meant, but He did not explain.

"He must mean land for our developments," I thought, my

mind on material things. Business had prospered as I traveled across the country preaching the gospel. John Wheeler and I had started a new corporation, 3:20 Builders, Inc. (named after Revelation 3:20) and 3:16 Investments (named after John 3:16). Mansion Homes began. In another deal, we bought some townhouses in Houston. Business was very good. It seemed as though God was blessing everything we touched. But I kept hearing the words of Jesus: "I have called you to preach My Bible to all the world."

As I was driving down Memorial Drive, the rain was just pouring down. Water splashed out in sheets as cars passed one another on the road. Every once in a while there was a flash of lightning, followed by a booming peal of thunder.

As I drove along I hummed, watching the traffic. The windshield wipers slapped the rain away. Suddenly, with no warning at all, I heard God's audible voice.

"Chris Panos, just as I called John the Baptist to proclaim the first coming of Jesus Christ, so I have called you to proclaim Christ before He returns again."

Tears rolled down my cheeks. I tried to speak, but I couldn't get any words past the lump in my throat. As the tears continued, I couldn't see to drive. I pulled off onto the shoulder.

In the following months, I threw myself into study. I continued to read the Bible. I prayed more. I listened to sermons preached by great men of God. I read books by Moody, Booth, Finney, Torrey, Wigglesworth, Price, Bosworth, Osborn, and Cerullo. I had tapes of some of Billy Graham's sermons, and I played them over and over again, even counting the words he used in order to learn his unique way of presenting the gospel.

As Easter approached that year, I felt a growing sense of anticipation. I knew God was preparing to launch me into a world-wide ministry. Soon, Costa Deir came to town. Costa and I had been friends for some time and I knew he had an apostolic ministry both here and abroad.

"Chris," Costa said, "I am going to Jerusalem and Europe on a preaching mission this Easter. Why don't you come along?"

I'm not sure Costa actually expected me to take him up on that offer, but I did. Before we left, I had a talk with my partner, John Wheeler.

"I think God is leading me into full-time ministry," I told him. "We have good people working for us. Things are going well enough for you to get along without me, if you have to. If God gives me the confirmation, I may be getting out of business altogether."

I hadn't decided anything as yet, but I wanted my business partner to be aware of what was going on.

Costa and I went to Egypt, Israel, Lebanon, Jordan, and Greece. We had some memorable times on that trip, but as far as the ministry went, it was disappointing to me. In America, I was used to speaking to large crowds. We spoke to groups of five and ten, and almost without exception, those fives and tens were already born again. God has given Costa a demanding and specialized ministry to stabilize and strengthen leadership wherever he goes, especially in the Middle East. But, I began to recognize, that was not my call. I wanted to save souls. But how could you save souls, if you only talked to Christians?

Somehow, some day, I planned to find a way to reach the sinners. And not just five or ten at a time, either. As Costa and I continued to travel, I began to pray more and more often the prayer that has become a lifelong petition, "Lord, give me souls."

Chapter Thirteen
Sell It All

After my trip with Costa, I was restless. Although I threw myself into my work, the work wasn't satisfying. I was eager to be out winning souls, but didn't see how I was going to go about it. Neither did Earnestine.

Both Earnestine and I had met people who lived on faith, who had no fixed source of income, but simply trusted God to send in the money to provide for their needs. But it was one thing to hear about it, and another thing to do it. If we were going to live on faith, first we needed the faith to live on.

During that time, Earnestine worried about how we would be supported if I gave up my businesses. I worried about knowing God's will. I was sure in my own heart that "where God guides, He provides," but I was worried that I might be getting ahead of the Lord. I didn't know if living on faith was His will for us at that time or not.

I continued to pray and seek God's will. Then, in June, 1966, I ran across the story of Praying Hyde. Hyde had been a man who "prayed always," often spending whole nights in prayer. I was excited. I couldn't imagine anyone praying for so long at a time. The thought nagged at me. Soon it became a challenge. I wanted to see if I could do it too.

"Earnestine," I said, "I can't see how it's possible to pray all night. But Praying Hyde did it. If he did it, maybe I can do it. I'm going to try it this Fourth of July and see if I can spend twenty-four hours in fasting and prayer."

I told Earnestine and the children that the living room was off-limits that day. Early that morning, I went into the living room and began my vigil. I prayed a long time, read the Bible, meditated, and praised the Lord. Morning changed to afternoon, and afternoon to evening. I prayed on. Sometime in the middle of the night, my eyes fell upon a copy of T.L. Osborn's *Faith Digest*. I had read his books, but was unfamiliar with his magazine. I picked it up and began to read. The lead story told how T.L. Osborn had failed as a missionary to India in the earlier part of his ministry, before going on to his later successes. I was strangely moved by the account. I began to weep and cry out, "Lord, send me! Send me!"

As I continued to weep and cry out, the Lord walked into that living room and stood behind me. I was awestruck. I could actually feel His presence on my back. The room filled with a sound like the fluttering of many wings.

"Son, take up your pen and write," He said. I grabbed a pen and began to take down the words as He spoke them, a phrase at a time.

"Not many days hence, you will receive a letter. Fear not. It is an invitation to go to India and preach the gospel to the lost. You will be there for ninety days.

"Be not afraid, for I am with you. You have cried, 'Lord, I want to preach the gospel in all the world.' So shall it come to pass. As I was with Moses, with Joshua, with Price, and with Osborn, so shall I be with you. Only believe."

I seemed to be floating in the heavenlies, though I was aware that I was still in my living room. I rejoiced.

Then the Voice came again. "Write these words. Sell all and go, for I am with you." It was the mandate I'd been waiting for.

I wondered how Earnestine was going to take the news. I didn't have long to wait. I had prayed almost all night—a miracle in itself—and the Lord had visited me just before dawn. Soon Earnestine woke up.

"Earnestine," I told her, "I had a visitation from the Lord last night. I'm going to go to India to preach the gospel. And that's not all! We're going to live on faith. The Lord told me to sell everything we have."

"Sell everything we have!" She was shocked. "What are we going to live on? Where are we going to live?" She looked around at her luxurious modern kitchen, and the spacious living room.

"Do we have to sell the house?" she asked.

"Honey, the Lord said, 'Sell all and go, for I am with you.' He'll take care of us."

Earnestine looked unconvinced.

I was tired from the lack of sleep, but anxious to get started. I called John Wheeler, who was a partner in one of my business ventures, and told him I had to see him at the office immediately.

As soon as I got there, I told him the news. "John, do you remember how I told you I might be getting out of the building business? Well, the Lord spoke to me last night. He told me to sell all and go, and preach. John, I want to get out of the building business."

"Listen to reason," John said. "If you'll stay with us, we can work out our partnership so you can preach the gospel too. If you want to preach, preach, but stay with us. You can preach all over the world if you'll just come back to Houston at least one week every six weeks."

It sounded like a good deal. Six weeks was forty-two days. But the Lord had said I'd be in India for ninety days.

"I appreciate your offer, but it just won't work," I said, thinking of the ninety days.

"Oh, yes it will!" he said. "If you'll agree, you can help us put the big deals together and work out the arrangements. If you'll just come back to Houston one week out of six weeks, we'll pay you $26,000 a year, plus one per cent of all the deals you package for us. We'll even give you a clause to protect your salary against inflation."

The agreement was very attractive. But I knew I had to obey God.

"No, John, God told me to sell everything, and that's what I have to do. Call the attorneys and sell me out," I told him. It was the hardest decision I ever made.

Just as I finished signing the papers selling out my interest, the secretary came in.

"Mr. Panos, your wife is on the phone," she said.

"Chris?" Earnestine's voice sounded shaky. "I've got to take Chrissy to the hospital. He got hit on the back of his head by a swing, and it's like he's been scalped. The hair and skin have been peeled back. All you can see is blood and bone."

"I'll meet you at the emergency ward," I told her. Praying, I drove to the hospital. By the time I got there, the doctors had stitched Chrissy's scalp in place. His head was bandaged. In time, it healed perfectly. I didn't have the faith then to pray for instantaneous healing, the way I would today, but I learned one important lesson from that incident. When something goes wrong, it isn't necessarily because you're out of the will of God. Sometimes, it may mean that you're in it, and the devil's mad at you. He ought to be, he's on the losing side!

Sell It All

Earnestine was close to tears. She isn't a crying person, but her secure world was being threatened. "Chris," she asked me, "are you sure you know what you are doing?"

"Just as sure as can be," I said.

"Well, I'm not sure," she told me. "I just don't feel called by God to give up my home. And what about the children? What about things like piano lessons for Georganna? And college? We've always planned to send them both to college. When you sell the rest of your business, and if you sell the house, won't you at least set aside some money for the children's education?"

It was another test. I knew that John Wheeler's offer to me had been God's way of testing me to see if I would give up my ambition to make a million dollars. Now He was testing me again only this test was more subtle. He was checking to see if He really came first in my life—even before the children I loved. I remembered the story of Abraham and Isaac. Abraham had been willing to kill his only son in order to obey the Lord. Surely I could give up my dreams of a college education for mine, if it were necessary. I didn't think it would be. I was sure that the Lord would provide for Georganna and Chrissy to go to college when the time came.

"Earnestine," I told her, "I have to obey God. God said He would provide. He said He would be with me. I know He will take care of us."

Earnestine looked unconvinced, and she remained unconvinced during the months that followed. The Lord had told me that "not many days hence" a letter would arrive from India—but no letter came. Meanwhile, I had put our house on the market, sold my businesses, and given the money away to missionaries and others in God's work. We lived on the fees and offerings from my preaching engagements.

About six months after my all-night prayer session, the letter from India came. I didn't open it; instead, I went into the bedroom where Earnestine was sitting, and handed the battered blue aerogram to her.

"Before you open it," I told her, "I can tell you what it is. It's that invitation to preach in India, just like God said."

"Are you sure this is right?" Earnestine asked. "Are you sure of all this? Please, for my sake and the sake of the children, be sure this is God's will."

I was sure, but this living by faith wasn't as easy as I had thought it would be. I thought of the businesses I had sold, the success to which I'd waved goodbye with just a few quick strokes of my pen. Six months ago, I had had a payroll of $50,000 a month. Now I had almost nothing.

As if reading my thoughts, Earnestine said, "You used to give me a thousand dollars a month for bills and household expenses. This month, you gave me twenty-five. That's quite a drop. I just don't see how we're going to make it. And how are you going to get the money to go to India?"

I didn't see how we were going to make it, either, but I knew that we would. During the past month, we'd been so poor that if my parents hadn't had us over to dinner fairly often, there were times when we might have had to go hungry. But the point was, I reminded myself, that we *hadn't* gone hungry. God had used my parents to provide for us.

"God will provide," I told Earnestine, motioning for her to open the letter.

The letter was from Apostle P.M. Samuel of India.

"I was praying early the morning of July 5," he wrote, "and the Lord impressed me to invite you to come to our conference in India. The needs here are great. More than five hundred churches are under our guidance. We need your help."

I was filled with awe. The Lord must have spoken to Apostle Samuel the very night He'd spoken to me! I had met

Apostle Samuel here in Houston, at a friend's house, but he knew me only as a businessman. He knew nothing of my call to preach, except whatever the Lord might have revealed to him. For him to write and invite me to preach at a conference was such a miracle that it stunned me. I was astounded at the way God works.

As I prayed about the trip, God impressed me that I was to go with Ray Jennings, a missionary to India. I got him on the phone and introduced myself.

"Ray, God has told me I will go to India with you in a few days."

There was a long pause on the other end of the line. Finally he said, "That's amazing. Yesterday a woman came up to me in a meeting. She said I would go with a dark-haired man on the trip. What color is your hair?"

"Nice and dark," I told him.

Chapter Fourteen
Next Stop: Prague

People thought I was crazy when I said I'd been called to preach. Friends called to try to convince me that I'd missed my calling. They told me that I was "supposed" to be in business, making money to support God's work. I didn't worry. I knew what had happened in the hospital. I remembered the time God spoke to me on Memorial Drive. Fresh in my mind was the memory of the early morning of July 5, and the miraculous way God had worked out all the details of the trip.

I was cheered, too, by a letter personally delivered by John Wheeler. "I believe in your work," he began. "I believe God has called you to be a minister to the world." Included was his check for $7,000.

It wasn't long before I'd given away most of the money. There were too many missionaries and preachers who needed help. I couldn't sit by and let them be needy, not while I had that much money in my pocket. I knew there would be more where that came from. God would supply my needs and the needs of my family, but He expected me to share my abundance with my brothers and sisters who were in need.

I was so sure God would supply that I left Earnestine with only a few hundred dollars to last her ninety days. "God will provide," I told her. "He always has and He always will."

Shortly after I left, she received a large (and unexpected) income tax refund in the mail. I had left her with the task of having our remaining possessions moved into an apartment, as we had sold our house shortly before I left. The check was very welcome. Earnestine used the money to cover some incidental moving expenses, and to live on until I returned.

Ray and I flew to New York to board our sleek Air India jetliner. We dozed and chatted as the plane soared across the ocean, heading towards London's Heathrow Airport. We refueled and took off again almost immediately for our next stop, Czechoslovakia.

"You must be very circumspect," Ray told me as we began our descent into the Prague airport. "This is a Communist country, and the government is against all religion. Most of the airport personnel in these Communist countries are actually secret agents. They're very hard on people who talk about Christ."

Ray kept checking his pockets time and again to make sure his papers were in order. At that time, the papers were full of stories about travelers who had been arrested by the Communists for one reason or another. I checked my papers and then I prayed, binding the principalities and powers.

When we left the plane, two Communist guards came walking up the ramp towards us as we were walking down. We were right in their path.

"Move aside, you," one of them grunted. He waved the muzzle of his machine gun to point the way.

"Move aside yourself!" I told the startled guard. "If you want to get by, go around."

I stood stock still. Ray turned pale.

The guard looked steadily at me. Finally, he walked around me and headed toward the airplane.

Ray was upset. "Chris, you can't act like that here! Don't you know you could get arrested for pulling a stunt like that?"

"Listen, Ray," I explained, "I just didn't have any witness from God to move out of his way. I am God's servant. That guard serves the prince of darkness. I just don't see how it will glorify the Lord for me to be bluffed by him."

Ray never knew I had been scared stiff while I was standing up to the guard. I didn't have any witness to admit that either!

Both of us were relieved when we boarded the white Air India plane again and headed out of Czechoslovakia. We ate and dozed again as we soared towards India. It was dark when we landed. After clearing customs, we climbed into the taxi for the ride to the hotel.

It was some ride! The Indian taxi driver tore off into the countryside, with his lights off. As we sped down the road, I held my breath and prayed that we'd reach the hotel safely. At the rate we were going, it wasn't long before my prayer was answered. Suddenly, the taxi driver rounded a corner, turned on his lights, and pulled into a square. All across the square, people lay sleeping. Many of them were covered only by dirty rags or a piece of burlap sack. Some had only the clothes on their backs for shelter. Row after row they lay there—old people, infants, and middle-aged. It was my first exposure to the poor of India, and I couldn't believe my eyes. Or my nose. The stench was incredible.

"Don't they have homes?" I asked Ray.

"This *is* their home," he said. "A generation or two ago, yes, maybe they had homes. Then maybe there was a famine, or maybe the family land got just too small to be divided any more. So they came to the city to find a job, but with no education and no skills to offer, there simply are no jobs to be had. The job market here is glutted with unskilled labor. These people are happy to do even the most menial tasks. Some poor women make their living just by following a cow or water buffalo around and gathering its dung. They mix the dung with straw and sell the cakes to use as fuel after drying them in the sun. Over half the population of India lives like this—without even a tent for shelter."

As we threaded through the sleeping forms towards the hotel, a mutilated hand was stretched in our direction.

"Baksheesh, baksheesh," the man murmured.

"He's asking for alms," Ray said. "Do you see how his fingers are worn to stumps? He's a leper. Hindu families just throw their lepers out. There are few leprosariums. They believe in reincarnation, so they feel that anyone with leprosy is just getting what he deserves. They believe he had to have been a very wicked person in his past life, in order to deserve to become a leper."

Ray had lived many years in India as a missionary. He was a mine of information, most of it heartbreaking.

In the morning we were picked up and driven to P.M. Samuel's house, where we were to stay. It was close to the huge Vijayawada convention at which I would be speaking. Thousands of Indian Christians attend this convention, meeting together to worship God and to be renewed spiritually.

My first sermon in India was one that I'd used before. It had as its theme the story of the Roman centurion in Matthew 8. Even as I spoke, I could sense in my spirit that some of the leaders of the meeting were disturbed. They

frowned—and I was using my best sermon! It was discon-
certing.

But no matter how disquieted I felt, I knew that the
sermon exalted God. Sure enough, the power of God fell
across the congregation and people were saved and healed.

There were about fifteen thousand people in the crowd.
By the time I had finished my sermon, many former cripples
had crowded towards the front of this area, often carrying
their now-useless crutches and canes aloft. As I gave the
invitation for people to accept Jesus, five thousand hands
went up.

God's power had fallen in a mighty way. The blind saw, the
deaf heard, cripples walked, and thousands were saved. I
was awed by the power and glory of God. But despite all this,
some of the leaders were waiting for me after the meeting.

"Brother Panos," the spokesman said, "we do not believe
in preaching from prepared notes and we were unhappy that
you used notes to preach from."

So *that* explained the frowns I had seen on the platform! I
was astounded.

"What difference does it make?" I asked.

"We do not think that the Spirit can move freely when a
man does not preach extemporaneously. We believe that the
Holy Spirit is hampered by notes."

I was too tired to argue. I returned to P.M. Samuel's
house, upset by the whole incident. In my heart I knew the
important thing was that the gospel had been preached and
God had honored His word.

The convention closed, but I continued to preach in con-
ferences, conventions, churches, revivals, and parks all over
the area.

India had gotten to me. I was aghast at the poverty, the
spiritual darkness, the sickness and the hunger—both
spiritual and physical—that I saw around me. In the spirit, I

agonized over the situation. I was conscious of my own inadequacies. I needed God's help. When I was not actually at a meeting, I spent most of my time fasting and praying.

One morning during this period, I had gone up to the roof of the house where I was staying. The houses in that area have flat roofs, and people use them the way we'd use a terrace. There, alone, except for God and one solitary raven, I prayed. I was desperate to hear from God.

"If God can talk through a donkey to Balaam," I said to myself, "He can talk through a raven to me. After all, didn't a raven bring food to Elijah, when he was hungry?" I decided it was worth a try.

"Lord, speak to me through this raven," I prayed. "Raven, speak in the name of Jesus!"

"Awwwk!" croaked the raven. And I did not receive the interpretation.

I had been impatient, wanting God to speak to me then and there. But God, who is never impatient, chose a later time in which to speak. That evening, I was sitting with the other speakers on the platform, waiting for the evening service to start. I had my head bowed in prayer, so I didn't see what was going on, but someone described it to me later.

Out of nowhere, a tall, dark-skinned man, one of the well-known Christian prophets of the area, came striding through the crowd. He headed straight for the platform and came to where I was seated. As I sat there praying with my eyes closed, I felt someone lay his hands on my head. A strong voice spoke out in an Indian dialect. One of the interpreters translated the message as the prophet spoke.

"Thus saith the Holy Ghost: 'You will go into every nation and take My gospel. You will stand before kings. You will speak to multitudes, and you will go into nations that only a few will dare to enter.

" 'Your life will be in constant danger. Fear not, for I am

with you. I will strengthen you. Yea, I will uphold you with the right hand of My righteousness. Go.

" 'You shall not fear but speak the words I will put within your mouth. I will confirm the word that you speak, for it shall not be your words, but My words.

" 'Go now and be My servant, for as of this day the anointing shall flow through your life and signs and wonders shall follow you every step of the way.' "

The tall Indian added many details of my early life and even mentioned things that I'd forgotten! I was stunned, flabbergasted, overjoyed. What a miracle!

After the prophecy, the crusades and meetings continued for several weeks. Soon, though, I began to believe God was telling me that it was time to leave. I told my hosts. To this day, I am convinced that they thought I was leaving too early—especially after a prophecy like that.

"I am sorry," I told them, "but I have to leave. God has somewhere else for me to go."

Chapter Fifteen
God's Spy

God had a few stops for me to make on my way home from India. The first was Tel Aviv, where I made a quick stopover before going on to Athens. The atmosphere in Israel was tense. Everyone knew the Arabs were preparing for war, but nobody knew when or where they would attack. I stayed overnight at the YMCA and dined with a young couple from the Philippines.

"There is going to be a great change here," I told them as we ate. "Things aren't going to be the same."

Only a few months later, the Israelis defeated the Arabs in the Six Day War, retaking the holy city of Jerusalem and capturing much new territory.

After dinner I went straight to bed. I was exhausted. The crusades, the heat, and the bad food I had encountered in India had left me feeling weak and drained. The following morning I boarded a flight for Athens. The flight was short and pleasant. I could hardly wait to get there.

As the plane approached the airport, I noticed that

111

Athens was hemmed in on one side by the ocean, and on the others by mountains. Everything seemed to shine: light sparkled off the ocean and glistened from the brilliant white of the Parthenon, which was visible atop the Acropolis.

When we landed I checked into the Electra Hotel. On the way, we passed many of the little two-story houses that comprise so much of Athens. They look somewhat shabby by American standards, but I was so happy to be in Greece I didn't care. As soon as I had a chance, I climbed Mars Hill and looked out over the city, remembering how the Apostle Paul had preached from this very hill.

The Bible tells us that as Paul waited for Silas and Timothy in Athens, "his spirit was stirred in him, when he saw the city wholly given to idolatry." As I stood there, I wept, begging the Lord to save the souls of my countrymen.

Then, the Lord told me that there was about to be a change of government in Greece. The king would be overthrown; the colonels would come to power. I spoke that night in a little Greek church. I had barely begun to preach when the Lord impressed me to stop and tell the congregation what He had told me.

"God has told me something," I said to the people. "The government of Greece is going to change. The king will be overthrown. The army will march in the street. The church will lose its authority."

The people were stunned and whispered among themselves. I waited a moment, then finished my sermon. That night we drove to northern Greece, and I spent the following day with Christians from another Greek church. I preached again, with no intention of repeating the prophecy. I didn't need to: the word had spread, and the whole neighborhood was talking about the news. But as soon as I started my sermon, I was again impressed to stop. Again, I gave God's message of political upheaval. I did not dwell on the prophecy, not knowing when it would come to pass. Some prophecies take centuries before they are fulfilled. But that very night, tanks rumbled through the Athenian streets, and the city was awakened by sporadic gunfire. The next morning everybody awoke to find that the colonels had taken over, and a junta was in power. The king was exiled. The things God showed me had come to pass.

Guards stood around as I caught my airplane for Frankfurt, Germany, a few days later. I watched them, knowing that Greece was in for hard times. Unless Greece bows its knee to God, giving Him His rightful place, the country is ripe for a Communist takeover.

In Frankfurt, I stayed with a couple named Loffert. I had been given the Lofferts' name when I was in India, and we liked each other immediately. Mrs. Loffert makes the best cheesecake in the world, and she became a kind of second mother to me. I spoke in their church, and was well received by their little congregation. But I was restless.

"God has laid a burning desire on my heart to go to East Berlin," I told the Lofferts. They protested, but I stood firm. "I feel that I must go."

West Berlin is only a short hop by plane from Frankfurt. The weather was very nice as I got out of the airplane. Germany had just finished a long, hard winter, and the Berliners were happy about the coming of spring. I was happy too. I headed toward Checkpoint Charlie, the famous entry to East Berlin through the Berlin Wall. I got in line for the immigration check, mindful that I had two Bibles in my blue suitcase.

When my turn came, the surly guard eyed the two bags I was carrying. "Do you have any gifts?" he asked me.

"No," I replied.

The guard unzipped one bag and checked its contents.

"What do you have in here?" he asked me, touching the other bag.

Seized with a sudden inspiration from God, I answered, "Nothing but personal items." I shoved the bag at him. "But go on, check it all you want."

The guard just looked at me. Then he waved me on, casually stamping a clearance on both bags. I was through the checkpoint!

I walked out of the small, grim building and stood on the curb, catching my breath. A small white car in the bay near the entry caught my eye. Guards swarmed around it, slowly and methodically taking it apart and looking in every conceivable place for contraband. They had even pulled the seats out of the vehicle.

I walked over to the driver, who looked like an American. "What are they doing?" I asked him.

Exasperated, he replied, "Checking. Just checking. I've been here for hours, watching them go through this routine."

We stood by the car and watched as the soldiers continued their maddeningly slow inspection. My new acquaintance turned out to be an American from New York City. Finally, they started to put the car back together again. When they released it, the driver invited me along.

"How about some dinner?" he asked me. "I know a place nearby where they have fantastic Hungarian food. All this waiting has made me hungry."

I agreed, and we drove towards the restaurant.

My friend was right: the food was fantastic. As we ate, my friend asked the waiter for a beer. "Care to join me?" he asked.

"No, thanks," I told him. "I've been delivered."

"Delivered?" he asked. "What does that mean?"

"I used to be a drunk. It nearly ruined my life—that, and some other things. But I don't need it any more." I continued my testimony, telling him how Jesus Christ had saved me. "I did it the hard way," I said. "Jesus Christ literally had to let me break my thick skull in an automobile accident before I was ready to listen to Him. But there's an easier way. Would you like to receive Him as your Savior now?"

My new friend bowed his head. Thousands of miles from home, seated in a Hungarian restaurant in East Berlin, my friend from New York invited Jesus Christ to come into his life. He was won to the Lord in enemy territory! His face shone as he raised his head.

After dinner, we parted company, and I checked into a small, cheap hotel in the Communist zone.

As I prayed that night, I asked the Lord what He wanted me to do. I was tired, and I missed my family. Part of me wanted to go home and see my wife and children; the other part wanted to stay and spread the light of the gospel in this country that was full of all-too-evident darkness.

"I am ready to do whatever you want me to do," I told Him, "but please make your will known to me. I need to know what you want me to do."

The answer didn't come that night, but it was not long in coming. The next morning, impatient to be getting on with things, I decided to try an experiment. Although the official East German policy was to issue permits only for twenty-four or seventy-two hours, I had heard that a few special people were sometimes able to obtain 120-day visas. If God were in my wanting to stay. He would provide a 120-day visa for me. If not, then it probably was His will for me to go home.

When I went to the immigration office, the German behind the desk looked at me as though I were crazy.

"I want a visa," I had told him. "I want to stay ninety—no,

make that 120 days—in Eastern Germany."

He shook his head at me and turned away, probably thinking something derogatory about the crazy American standing in his office.

"No, I mean it," I told him. "I want a 120-day visa."

He spat out a single word: "Impossible!"

I insisted. He became conciliatory, treating me like a slightly retarded child.

"I am very sorry, but it is impossible for you to get a 120-day visa. We can get you a twenty-four hour pass, or a seventy-two hour permit, but to stay longer is impossible. It isn't allowed."

"I want to see your boss," I told him.

This seemed to strike him as a good idea. It was one way to get rid of this crazy foreigner. He showed me into a little office and introduced me to another official. I repeated my request. He denied it.

"I want to see your boss," I told him.

I went higher and higher up the ladder, finally coming to the chief of the East Berlin area.

"What do you do?" this man asked me.

"I am a teacher," I told him.

"What do you teach?"

"Things people ought to know."

"What kind of things?"

"None of your business," I replied, looking straight at him.

The man looked puzzled at my answer and my attitude. He looked down and shuffled some papers, thinking.

"Where do you intend to go?" he asked me after a moment.

"Anywhere I can, teaching," I replied.

The questions and answers went on for some time, touching on this and that. Finally, we came to the end of the questions and I received a 120-day visa.

"Thank you, Father," I said, holding the precious visa tenderly. It was a gift from God. "Thank you."

I spent the day in East Berlin, talking to people about Jesus, passing out tracts, witnessing. Towards the end of the afternoon, I was walking down a long, empty street and praying.

"I am ready to die for you," I told the Lord. "I am ready to stay wherever you want me to be. I am your man." I wept as I consecrated my life to Him again.

As I walked, the Lord interrupted my thoughts. "You have been telling Me that you are willing to die for Me, but you are not ready to die for Me yet. It is not your time to die yet. If I ask you to give Me a cup of cold water, then I will first give you that water. If I ask you to die, then I will first prepare you to be a martyr. But you don't have to die. It is not your time. It is your time to go home."

"But the visa!" I exclaimed. "Lord, I don't understand." And He didn't explain.

Back at the hotel, I made ready to leave, and passed back through the border to West Germany the following morning. Next, I made the short hop by air to Frankfurt and went to the Lofferts'. We had a joyous reunion, and I told my hosts of my adventures. I was ready to return to Houston, but I had one short errand to do before I got back.

I enlisted the Lofferts' help and we gathered some German New Testaments. Before I went back to Houston, I wanted to smuggle the gospel into East Germany, leaving it where it would do the most good while I went back to the States. I stuffed my suitcases full and went to the Frankfurt ticket office.

As I was making flight arrangements, I ran into the Filipino couple again. Having visited Israel, they were now touring Europe on their vacation.

"Would you like to go with me to East Berlin?" I asked them.

"Yes, we would, very much," the man replied. "But we cannot return to the Philippines if we have a Communist stamp on our passports."

"Come on. I will take care of the passports at the border," I said. My God could do anything—even fix a passport.

Our shuttle flight left a few hours later. It was a balmy spring day when we got into West Berlin. I had planned to enter East Berlin via Checkpoint Charlie, but suddenly felt impressed to use another route.

"We'll take the S-Bahn," I told the Filipinos, steering them towards the train station. We boarded the train and disembarked at the border.

The checkpoint was dark and oppressive. Dim light bulbs hung in the dingy gray corridors. I headed toward the check station, followed by the Filipinos.

The guard opened our passports and looked at them. He turned on his high stool and handed them back through a slot in the wall. There was a man back there, but all we could see were his eyes. Suddenly the Lord showed me what to do.

"No stamp passports," I said, banging my hand on the wooden counter. The startled guard jumped back.

"NO STAMP PASSPORTS!" I shouted again, banging my fist down. The man behind the slot handed our passports back to the guard.

The guard picked up his heavy stamp and put the passports on the inkstained counter. He applied the stamp to its pad, making sure it was thoroughly inked. He looked at me. I looked back. Then he applied the stamp to blank sheets of paper and handed all three passports back to me unstamped.

The Filipinos were pale underneath their brown complex-

Chris Panos, 1997

To Chris Panos
with best wishes   *signature: Gy Bush*

George Bush, US President, with Chris
Panos at the Govenor's Ball, China.

Indira Gandhi with Chris Panos, New Delhi, India, Nov. 28, 1979.

Appearing left to right: Chris Panos, Archbishop Makarios, Pat Robertson, Harrald Bredesen, 1974.

ions. It was hours before the wife stopped shaking. She shook and trembled till we parted company, but seemed relieved that the ordeal was behind her. I was relieved myself. I have often wondered if the Lord didn't use that 120-day visa (something usually reserved for Communist VIPs) to influence the guard not to stamp my passport when I shouted at him. But I probably never will know what went through his mind until I get to heaven—and by then I probably won't care.

On our way out of customs, we had to walk on down a concrete tiled corridor. There were no doors, but guards were stationed up and down the hallway. Ahead of us, there was a sudden commotion. There was a shout of fear, a cry of pain. Two burly guards roughly grabbed a woman and a little boy, pulled them into an open cubicle near the inspection point and shoved them down onto a rough wooden bench. The woman cringed in fear as guards seized her suitcase. The boy grabbed his mother's arm and sobbed, his face buried in the sleeve of her coat.

"What's going on?" I asked one of the guards.

"They're arresting the little boy," he told me. "He was trying to smuggle in a comic book."

"A comic book?"

"Yes," he told me smugly, "a decadent Western comic book." He looked pleased.

"Look what you've gotten yourself into now!" a familiar voice told me. It was the devil again. "They don't play around here. They're arresting that little boy because he smuggled in one comic. What do you think they'll do to you when they catch you with a whole suitcase full of Bibles? I'll tell you what they'll do: they'll stick you so far back they'll have to have a map to find you."

I was scared. My palms were sweaty. But only for a minute—then I got mad. "Shut up," I told the devil. "You are lying again. I belong to Jesus, and in His name I bind you, and all your evil powers, principalities, spirits of wickedness, and rulers of darkness. I forbid you to hinder me in any way."

Then I grabbed the guard. "What are you doing?" I shouted. "I want you to understand we are foreigners. I am an American citizen. We are not used to seeing people treated this way. You ought to be ashamed of yourself, manhandling that woman.

"Why do you treat people this way? Who do you think we are? Lunatics? Criminals? What's wrong with you?"

I got angrier and angrier as I screamed at the startled guard. People stared in our direction. Even the guards with the woman and the small boy were looking in our direction. Everyone acted like they couldn't believe their ears.

I drew a deep breath, preparing to shout again. The guard grabbed me, and pushed me along the line. "Pass on through. Please," he said, anxious to quiet the source of the commotion. I moved on into East Germany with the Filipinos, the Bibles safe in my suitcase.

Although the Filipinos soon returned to West Germany, I spent two glorious days witnessing, passing out tracts, and New Testaments, and telling everyone who would listen how to receive Jesus as their Savior. I talked to anyone: chambermaids, houseboys, desk clerks, policemen, cab drivers, and waiters. I hardly had time to sleep, I was so excited with the doors God opened for me. All too quickly, however, I ran out of tracts and New Testaments, and the Lord began to tell me that it was time for me to head on home. I would have liked to stay, but He was the boss.

Still, I had made a start. Caleb and Joshua had spied out the land of Canaan for God's people when it was enemy territory. They had gone back to Moses and reported, "We are well able to take the land." I, too, had spied out enemy territory as one of God's spies. I had gone behind the iron curtain and found it was occupied by very real enemies. But like Caleb and Joshua, I was able to report that we are well able to take the land. There are no closed doors to the gospel.

Chapter Sixteen
The Mexican Episode

We had grease all over us.

Earnestine and I had been offered a little house to live in right after I got back, so we had moved out of the apartment. We had no stove. One was donated to us, but it was the greasiest, dirtiest, messiest stove you ever saw. The previous owner was a dear, sweet sister in the Lord, but she came from a country whose customs were different than ours. Those customs evidently didn't include cleaning kitchen ranges.

Earnestine took one look and shuddered. "Look at this. I'll never get it clean!" she said. If she was thinking about the beautiful, modern stove we'd left behind, she didn't mention it as we scrubbed away. I was depressed. What kind of life was this to offer my wife and family? I knew God had called me into the ministry. But here we were, covered with grease. It didn't seem right.

As I prayed, I became convinced that God wanted to supply our needs and that He hadn't called us to live in poverty. Certain verses kept coming to mind, verses like "my God shall supply all your need according to his riches in glory by Christ Jesus," and "Delight thyself also in the Lord, and he shall give thee the desires of thy heart." We began praying as a family for the things we needed in the house.

A minister friend brought over a used washing machine, and I turned it down. "Thank you for your love," I told him, "but I believe God will supply me with the best, 'according to his riches in glory.' I'm believing Him for a new washing machine."

He started to get mad. "Now, look, Chris—" he began.

"No, you look," I told him. "God is a great God. He'll answer our prayers in a great way."

We talked some more, then he got in the truck and drove away. A few hours later, the phone rang. It was another friend. He had $150 that he wanted to give to us. It was just enough to buy a brand-new washing machine. Just as I'd thought, God didn't want me to have to make do with second-best. I was giving Him the best I had; He was going to give me the best He had.

As I prayed and waited on the Lord, I became convinced my family should go with me on my next mission. Earnestine didn't want to go. She had two small children to think of, and she just didn't feel like God was calling her to take the children off to some primitive mission field, especially since we had so little money.

"It's one thing for you to go off on these missions, Chris," she said. "God has called you to go and preach the gospel. But He hasn't called me. Let me stay home and take care of the children here in America. I just don't feel like I've been called to that kind of life."

But I insisted. I had decided that we would all go next time.

My next assignment came as I preached at Lakewood

Church and told of my experiences in Greece, India, and East Germany. There was a missionary to Mexico in the meeting named Earl Kellum. He asked for my help and invited me to preach to the people there. I accepted his invitation enthusiastically and told Earnestine to get ready to go.

"Chris, where are we going to get the money?" Earnestine asked me. We had no money coming in and no expectation of any. By this time I had run up several thousand dollars' worth of debts, using my various charge cards as I traveled. But the door to Mexico was open. If God wanted me to go, He would pay for the trip.

The Lakewood Church members took up an offering and sent us to south Texas. I preached there, and we prepared to enter Mexico with a hundred dollars in cash and a gasoline credit card.

We traveled through northern Mexico, preaching wherever we could. As we headed in the direction of Vera Cruz, the country became more and more primitive. Earnestine had felt oppressed from the moment we crossed the border. Poverty and filth were everywhere, and on top of everything else, Georganna soon caught diarrhea. Many of the places we stopped at night had dirt floors and only holes for windows. Nearly all of our accommodations were dirty by American standards, and indoor plumbing was a rarity. In fact, one place we stayed at stands out in my memory because of the indoor plumbing. It had a unique system. The building perched on the top of a cliff, overhanging a gorge which had its bottom hundreds of feet below. When I entered the bathroom, I could feel a breeze—but there wasn't any window. Puzzled, I looked for the source of the air current. I found it in the toilet. When I looked through the hole in the seat, I got a bird's-eye view of the gorge below.

As we traveled, Earnestine became more and more depressed. The food was bad and the water was unsafe to drink. But it wasn't only our living conditions that were upsetting Earnestine—it was the condition of the missionaries we visited along the way. Many people have come to realize that an effective way to evangelize a country is to go in and teach the nationals how to preach the gospel themselves. And when missionaries do go into a country to live, most of them have learned how to claim God's provision for their needs by faith. Mexico is, for the most part, a very poor country. The missionaries lived in a state of poverty and oppression that appalled Earnestine. We were on a short-term trip and would soon be returning to all the comforts of home. But the missionaries *had* no comforts of home. Many of their houses were so dirty that they smelled. And often the missionaries seemed to be more interested in civilizing the Mexicans than in evangelizing them. They theorized that if they lived among the Mexicans long enough, their culture and religion would rub off on those around them. To us, it looked like the missionaries' battle plan often worked in reverse. Instead of civilizing the natives, the natives often "de-civilized" the missionaries.

Earnestine and I did what we could to bring the message of God's love to the missionaries as well as to the Mexicans. If we had just six dollars left, we'd spend all six to take a missionary couple to dinner, feed them Mexican steak and tell them that as children of the King they could believe God and He would supply many of the creature comforts they felt they had to do without.

Our travels took us to the foot of Pico Orisiba, the highest mountain in Mexico. At the foot of the mountain, we stopped at a Mexican-style motel. It had no glass in the windows, packed dirt for a floor, and outdoor plumbing, but it did have a little veranda where Earnestine could sit and watch the children as they played with the Mexican children in the courtyard.

"Earnestine, you're going to have to stay here with the children till I get back. There's just no way we can take them up the mountain. It gets cold up there, and we haven't brought warm clothing for them. You and the children keep praying for me while I'm up there," I said.

I knew Earnestine and the children would rather have come along, but even if they had had some warmer clothing, five-year-old Chrissy would have been too young to make the five-hour trek up the mountain. I left them with fifty cents (all the money we had left), a jar of peanut butter, and a box of crackers.

When Earl and I started up the mountain, I was glad I'd left Earnestine and the children behind. There was no road, only a small trail eighteen inches wide which snaked up the steep side. We climbed all day. The sun beat down mercilessly as we made our way higher, but eventually the clouds began to blow in from the Gulf of Mexico, which is not far from the snow-capped mountain. By the time we reached the village, a cold rainy wind was blowing.

"Oh, no," Earl said. "It's starting to rain. It's too late to go back down again, and now nobody will come out to hear you preach because of the rain."

I sought God, convinced that He would not lead us all the way up a mountain only to have a crusade ruined by a rainstorm. As we stood there, the rain began to fall in torrents. Leaves and debris scudded along in the wind, and rain slashed down so hard the drops stung when they hit. I continued to pray.

"My son," God said, "that they might see that I have sent you here to confirm My word with signs and wonders and miracles, speak out. Tell the people to walk out on their porches. Tell them to look up to heaven, to notice the cloudy skies and rain. Tell them the stars are going to shine."

I told Earl what God had told me, and asked him to translate.

"But Chris," Earl protested, "the people know it is raining."

"Tell them," I said.

Still he hesitated.

"God has commanded me to say this. Tell them exactly what I have said," I told him.

Earl began a less than enthusiastic translation.

"Tell them again."

He told them—with more zeal this time.

A few people came out on their porches. We were standing in the middle of the village, surrounded by thatched-roof houses and inundated by rain. The people watched as it pelted us. Suddenly—as suddenly as though someone had turned off a giant spigot in the sky—it stopped. We looked up.

"Look at that," I told Earl, pointing skyward. "There. And there. And there. And over there."

Awed, we watched as clouds blew away and brilliant stars shone in the deep blue sky. God had kept His word.

For a week I preached as Earl translated. The messages were followed by signs and wonders. People were healed and delivered, and accepted Jesus as their Savior.

Soon it was time to head back down the mountain. Earl and I took nearly a day to travel the steep and treacherous path down the mountain. The villagers had given us an offering of commodities: mostly poultry and some eggs. With Earl bartering in Spanish, we were able to exchange the offerings for money.

When I returned to the motel, I found that Earnestine and the children had had a rough time of it while I was gone. All they'd eaten that week was peanut butter and crackers. The peanut butter hadn't run out and they hadn't starved, but it was years before Earnestine could enjoy peanut butter again. But the Lord had laid it on the motel owner's heart to provide free soft drinks for Earnestine and the children—a real blessing in an area where the water wasn't fit to drink.

We paid off the motel bill and took Earnestine and the children out for a steak. The restaurant was out in the open—more like a canvas canopy than a building—and the steaks were typically Mexican. They had been pounded thin till they were each about twelve or fourteen inches long, and then covered with onions. We all thought that they tasted really good, although I suspect that Earnestine and the children would have liked anything at that point, so long as it wasn't peanut butter or crackers!

Later, when Earnestine and I were alone, Earnestine broke into tears. "Please, let's go home," she wept. "Please!"

I agreed, but began to pray that God would put a missionary fervor in Earnestine's heart. Soon, God let me know that He would take care of it—He would give Earnestine a burden for souls, like the one He had given me. I was confident that God would keep His promise. He had never failed me before.

Chapter Seventeen
Cold-Blooded Murder

Before we had left for Mexico, I had been approached about holding a series of meetings in Colombia. Now, as we headed home, I began to think about South America. The hardships we had encountered had discouraged Earnestine, but I was challenged. The first hurdle was, as usual, the money. If I was to go, I would have to believe God for the finances.

Earnestine and I began to pray that God would supply the money for me to go to Colombia. As we prayed, God showed me that He would send me $800 for the trip through a woman in south Texas. It wasn't long in coming. One day, shortly after we had returned home, the doorbell interrupted our daily devotions. It was the postman, with a special delivery letter from Victoria, Texas. When we opened it, it contained a check for $800, along with a note that it was to be used for a crusade to South America.

After contacting missionaries in Bogota, I left, not knowing when I would be back. The flight down was smooth and

enjoyable, now that God had delivered me from my fear of
flying. As soon as I landed, I got in touch with Mark Connor,
the missionary with whom I was to travel.

"The place where we are going is very hard," Mark said.
"The people are very opposed to *evangelismos*, as they call
us. A few of the women are faithful to God, but most of the
villagers continue to live in superstition, even though they
claim to be good Catholics. They don't want anyone coming
in to disrupt them, either. The last man who went in to
preach had one arm cut off, as a sign for others not to come.

I felt frightened, but I knew that God would protect me, as
He had behind the iron curtain. Still, I was on edge. Perhaps
this was good: it caused me to spend more time seeking God
and praying!

The morning after I met Mark Connor, he and I started off
in special vehicles, en route to a village just inside the jungle.
The trip was uneventful, but Mark's conversation was hair-
raising.

"Oh, by the way," he said, taking pains to keep his voice
casual, "yesterday some of the men of the village severely
beat a man who had been going to the Christian church.
They broke his leg and gave him a good going over. He is
very sick.

"It's always the men they attack," Mark continued.
"Never the women. They don't mind if a few 'foolish' women
attend church, but once the men start going, they have to
take it seriously. So they beat the men—or worse, sometimes."

I thought about this news as we drove through some of the
most beautiful countryside I have ever seen. The mountains
were covered in vivid shades of green, punctuated by water-
falls unlike any in America. Almost every shade of the rain-
bow was represented in the many tropical flowers, and even
in the insects. From a car, the Colombian jungle is gorgeous.

It is not so gorgeous if you have to walk through it, with the insects dropping on you from the trees. From the sanctuary of the car, however, we could enjoy the view, listening to the cawing and crowing of the multicolored parrots and other birds soaring through the trees.

As we approached the first stop on our itinerary, I thought about the preacher who had had his arm cut off, and the villager who had been so savagely beaten. "But I am trusting you, Father," I told the Lord.

When we stopped the car, a few women came out to greet us. They seemed very nervous and kept looking at the jungle growth surrounding the clearing where I was to preach. Mark feared for our safety. He kept a sharp eye on the thick jungle foliage.

We sang one song, but it was very weak. Rather than attempt another, I opened my Bible and began to preach. As I started my message, a stone whizzed by my head. It had been thrown very hard. More stones flew by, rattling through the trees behind us and puffing up dust near our feet. Mark turned to run, but I grabbed his wrist. Holding him in place, I prayed.

"Father, I claim your protection. In the name of Jesus, I bind the evil spirits and all the powers of darkness in this place." Then I turned to Mark. "Don't run," I said. "Stay right here. God has put you here to interpret for me. I am going to preach and you are going to interpret."

Almost immediately I was impressed to stop. I did. As I stood there, looking at the trees, most of the stones stopped coming. Only an occasional one whizzed by.

"I used to be just like you," I told the people behind the trees. I waved my hand towards the jungle to let the men know I was speaking about them. "I used to be a drunk. I used to want to kill people. I used to curse. I used to gamble."

I spoke slowly, phrase by phrase, and Mark translated, his voice gaining strength as he went along.

"Yes, I was just like you," I said.

There was silence. The stones stopped coming.

"Come in here," I shouted. This time, Mark shouted just like I did.

"Bring your rocks in here to the clearing. Bring your pistols, your guns, your machetes, your spears," I challenged them. "Don't be cowards—don't hide behind a bush. If you are going to kill me, then come in here and do it face to face. Don't hide out there in the jungles and do it. Don't be cowards—be men!"

One of the men stood up. He was dressed in ragged work clothes, but it wasn't the clothes that held my attention. It was the sharply-pointed, razor-edged, two-foot long machete that he carried in his right hand. Its point dragged the ground as he walked towards the clearing.

Other men followed him, each clutching a weapon. I saw pistols, rocks, sharp-pointed sticks, and a rifle or two. Mark breathed raggedly. Again, he was tensed up—but I had prudently continued to hold his hand fast in mine. He couldn't dash very far, dragging me along behind him.

"Stand fast," I told him. "God is with us."

The crowd looked sullen. The men had been challenged—they didn't like it.

"I am not here to start a new religion," I said. "I am not here to stop you from being good Catholics. The words I speak are not my words. No—I speak the words of God's Holy Spirit. God sent me here to your village in order that you might know Jesus, His Son. I want you to become good Catholics. If you were good Catholics, you would not have thrown rocks at me. If you were good Catholics, you would not have served the devil. But I am here to help you become better Catholics. I am here to help you become better men. I

am here to help you get full of the Holy Ghost and power."
A few of the men edged closer as I preached. Now they were listening intently. One of them threw himself on the ground, crying out in Spanish. I couldn't understand the words, but I knew he was crying out to God to save him.

I asked for the man who had been beaten, and one of the women went to a nearby hut to fetch him. Slowly, they approached the clearing. He dragged himself along, using two tree limbs as crutches. His leg was twisted awkwardly and dragged behind him. When he reached the clearing, he just propped himself up and stood there, his eyes downcast. It looked as though he was afraid even to look at the men who had done this to him.

"In the name of Jesus," I told him, "be healed!" I didn't even wait for Mark to interpret as I continued, "Throw down those crutches and walk!"

Instantly, the man straightened. His crutches fell to the ground. As we watched, his leg straightened and knit together, and the bruises began to yellow. His blackened eye opened. The eyeball turned white and the swelling went down. His eye looked as if it had never been damaged. The people watched in amazement.

"Hallelujah!" one woman shouted. Others shouted words in Spanish. I couldn't understand the words, but I could understand the spirit. They were praising God. Soon, every inhabitant of that village was kneeling in the clearing, their weapons forgotten in the dust. The entire village came to the Lord that day.

Mark and I went on to another village, leaving the people hungry to learn more about the Lord. Ordinarily, I would have stayed and taught, but since there were missionaries already in the area, I left this task to them. Mark and I went on into the jungle.

The mayor of the next village, Juan Ramiro, came out to

meet us, preparing to guide us the last few miles, where the trail led through the tall grass to his little village. His men preceded us, hacking a path through the grass with their machetes.

"*Hermano* Panos," Juan said, with a smile, "*Hermano*—" He tugged at my sleeve to get my attention. I stopped and looked at him.

He said something in Spanish, and I waited for Mark to interpret. "You must be very careful where you step," Mark said. Instinctively, I looked down at my feet. Ramiro laughed and continued, as Mark translated.

"You must be very careful. We have many snakes here in Colombia. Some of them are poisonous."

I shivered. I hate snakes as much as I hate spiders.

"But even though some are poisonous, the most prevalent are boa constrictors. Some of the boa constrictors grow as long as twenty feet. They can kill a horse." He pointed to a nearby tree. A thick greenish snake as thick as a man's arm slithered slowly through the tree.

"That snake could break the back of a horse by falling on him," Ramiro said. "Then he would swallow it. Snakes can swallow objects much larger than themselves. Their mouths are made differently than ours."

My skin crawled.

"You must be very careful or you'll step in a boa's mouth," Ramiro finished. He was rubbing it in, I thought. I remembered the words of Luke 10:19, "Behold, I give unto you power to tread on serpents and scorpions, and over all the power of the enemy: and nothing shall by any means hurt you."

"What did you say?" Mark asked me. I repeated the verse for him. He laughed, but looked somewhat relieved himself.

We forged ahead. I don't know about the others, but I was praying every step of the way. "Thou art my rod and my

136

staff. I will fear no evil," I said to the Lord, as we strode along the narrow path in the tough, head-high grass. We walked along, following the flashing machete blades ahead of us. Sweat rolled down our faces in the oppressive heat. After about two miles, we spotted a clearing in the jungle. It contained a small hut made of tree branches and palm fronds. A small, wrinkled woman lived there.

"*Hermano*," she shouted to me, "*Hermano.*" She motioned. In her hand was a cup of yellow liquid. She said something in Spanish, and Mark translated.

"She's offering you lemonade," Mark told me. He sounded amused.

"What's so funny?" I asked him.

"It was probably made with contaminated water and quite likely will make you sick. You'd better be careful." Mark was laughing at me, wondering what I'd do in this predicament.

I hesitated, but God's voice came in my ear. "Drink it, my son. She is offering you something that is very precious to her. Her offer means very much to her. Drink it."

Obediently, I drank the yellowish liquid, claiming the part of Mark 16:18 that says, "If they drink any deadly thing it shall not hurt them." I remained unharmed. I'd been vaccinated by a good shot of Mark 16:18!

That night was horrible. The hut was small and close. Mosquitoes filled the interior, and we used nets to keep them off. The heavy nets made breathing nearly impossible. The hut was roofed with dry palm leaves, which rustled all night with the sound of rats running across them. The rats were as big as tomcats, but few of them ventured inside the house for fear of the family "rat trap." This was actually a boa constrictor four feet long. The family didn't seem to like the boa constrictor any more than I did.

"It is a necessary evil," Mark explained to me. "Just put one of these ropes around your bed. The snakes won't crawl over it; they don't like the feeling of that rough, hairy rope scraping along their bellies."

All went well—or at least comparatively well—until the night that I forgot to put the rope around my cot before I went to bed. I had had a hard time falling asleep: the jungle birds screeched and squawked, the pumas and panthers howled and roared. It was hot and humid. Finally, I fell into a fitful sleep, only to awake just as the family boa started crawling up my leg. Because of the oppressive heat, I had worn only a pair of shorts to bed, and I could feel the snake's cool skin against mine. I was so frightened that without thinking of what I was doing, I grabbed the snake just below its head and squeezed with supernatural strength until it lay lifeless. It was the last time I ever forgot to put the rope around my bed.

Although the bad food, the tainted water, the heat, the rats, the boas, and the insects made living almost unbearable, I was filled with an inexplicable peace and joy in the midst of everything. Village after village responded to the word of God. Many were saved. Signs and wonders followed the preaching of the word. Eventually, however, Mark and I headed back towards Bogota.

On the way, we stopped at a small village church. I had begun to preach, when suddenly I received a word of knowledge.

"Where is Mary?" I asked. The congregation froze. Unknown to me, the woman named Mary was lying in a back room of the church, at the point of death from a cancer-like condition. Many of the people had been fasting and praying on her behalf.

"Bring Mary here," I said. "She's been healed." As I spoke, a large rat darted out of the room where Mary was and ran down the aisle and out the door. It was the ugliest-looking rat I'd ever seen—and by this time, I'd seen a lot of rats. As I watched it go, the Lord told me that it was a manifestation of the spirit of infirmity which had been about to kill Mary.

Some women went into the room where Mary had been lying, and brought her out. She was skin and bones, but she was walking under her own steam. After the service, I learned that her disease had caused many lesions on her skin—but these had already disappeared by the time I saw her. The little church rejoiced at the answer to its prayers.

Back in Bogota, I received a phone call. "Is this Chris Panos?" the caller wanted to know. "I heard about Mary. We need a man like you on the Amazon. Will you come?"

Quickly, I prayed. Yes, I would come.

I was startled when I met the man who'd called me. He looked like a pirate! He didn't have a patch over one eye, a bandanna around his head, or a single gold earring, but to me he looked like a pirate nevertheless. He was a big man, much taller than I was, with a large belly. He had a wicked-looking grin, but his heart was in the right place. He wanted to carry the gospel to the little villages along the Amazon. We went by boat. There was no other way to get there, but a boat just somehow seemed to suit him anyway.

"Do you see those?" he asked me, pointing to a school of small, harmless-looking fish. "They're piranhas. They're carnivores. They'd eat a horse if they got the chance. Wait till we make our next stop and I'll give you a demonstration."

At our next stop, he looked around till he found a boa constrictor curled around a tree. Its tail was on the ground; its head was lost up in the branches somewhere. Taking his machete, he started to slice the snake the way you might slice a loaf of French bread. Whack! Whack! Whack! Three foot-long sections of snake fell severed to the ground. He didn't stop. Whack! Whack! Whack! As he chopped, the top part of the boa constrictor slid helplessly into view, having lost the support of its tail. Soon, the boa was nothing but sections of snake meat. He carried some of these sections onto the boat with us as we set off again.

"Here, watch this" he told me, throwing a section of snake meat into the river. Instantly, the piranhas swarmed around it. Almost instantly, it was gone. Just—gone. He threw in another, then another. They vanished just as quickly.

"Hungry little creatures, aren't they?" he chuckled. "Don't dangle your fingers in the water!" His bloodthirsty laugh was in keeping with his piratical appearance. I was glad I was on good terms with him—I wouldn't have liked to have him for an enemy. I wondered just exactly what he'd been or done before he'd become a Christian, but I never did ask.

As we traveled along the Amazon, we preached in villages so remote that their primitive inhabitants wore little more than loin cloths. Some were cannibals. But primitive though they were, it didn't keep them from responding to the gospel and accepting Jesus as their Savior. The time passed very quickly. All too soon, I knew it was time for me to be heading home.

Chapter Eighteen
The House That Didn't Explode

Earnestine began to pray for a house of our own. She prayed this way for several years, even fasting for it on occasion. One morning, as she was reminding the Lord about this need, the Lord spoke to her and said, "If you want a house, why don't you give Me a chance to work?"

At first, Earnestine couldn't think what the Lord could possibly mean by this. Finally she decided that maybe—just maybe—He wanted her to take a step of faith and start looking for a house. We had absolutely no money at all to buy one with, but Earnestine decided to trust the Lord. Since it seemed as though she was always having to drive me to the airport—or pick me up there—Earnestine began to look in the neighborhood of Houston's International Airport. She looked and looked. Finally, after yet another afternoon of fruitless searching, Earnestine saw a realtor's "for sale" sign near a house she had been shown through.

When you've listed your house with a realtor, you're not supposed to show it on your own, but Earnestine was reluctant to make another trip to the same neighborhood.

"It's so small," Earnestine thought, "that it's probably not what we're looking for. But I'll just take a chance and see if they'll show it to me."

She rang the doorbell and explained her mission to the housewife who answered it.

"Come on in," the woman invited. "The realtor will only have this house two more weeks, anyway."

As Earnestine had suspected, the house *was* small—three small bedrooms, a combination dining-living room, a kitchen and attached garage. Also, it had no fireplace, and Earnestine had hoped to find a house that had one. As she thanked the woman and started to leave, the woman said, "By the way, we only want seven hundred dollars for our equity."

Earnestine was startled. Most homeowners had been asking prices in the thousands.

"We just want to get out," the woman explained. "We want to build a house. If this house doesn't sell, we'll just let it go back to the bank."

"Oh," Earnestine said, beginning to see the Lord's hand at work, "please don't do that. I'm just not sure if this is what I want, but please give us a call before you let it go back to the bank."

"All right," the woman said, "I will. But don't take too long to make up your mind. If the real estate company doesn't sell it, we're going to get rid of it right away."

Earnestine went home and prayed. During the next two weeks, the house remained unsold, despite the fact that all the other houses in that neighborhood were selling like hotcakes. Finally, the woman called to say that Earnestine had until the following Monday. On Monday, they were letting the house go back to the bank.

It was a Wednesday when the woman called Earnestine. On Thursday, a minister friend phoned me.

The House That Didn't Explode

"I'm speaking at a convention of Christian businessmen in Denver, Colorado, tomorrow," he said. "Do you want to come along?"

"Sure," I said. "When do we leave?"

As was becoming usual, I had to charge my plane ticket, but I felt led to go. And we did have a wonderful time. My friend spoke on Friday night, and on Saturday morning, I was asked to give a few words of testimony. I spoke for about five minutes. When I finished, I received a word of knowledge so spectacular that it surprised even me.

"Somebody has just received an eye healing," I stated. "You were blinded in an industrial accident, but the Lord has just given you a new pair of eyes."

"That's me!" a man called out. He hurried to the speaker's platform. "My eyes were so badly burned that the doctors said they looked just like raw hamburger," he said. "There was no hope of doing any kind of transplant. There just wasn't enough tissue for the doctors to work with. The whole colored part of my eyes had gone, and the whites were badly burned as well."

"Well," I said, "the whites look fine to me. And the irises are fine too. You have a bright new pair of beautiful blue eyes!"

"Blue?" he asked. "Did you say they were blue?"

"Yes, they're blue," I told him. "What did you expect?"

"They used to be brown," he said. "If what you say is true, this wasn't just an eye healing. The Lord really did give me a whole new pair of eyes."

I was overjoyed and so was everybody else. What a miracle!

"So this is why I was supposed to come," I thought. "What a blessing!" But the blessings hadn't finished yet. At the close of the meeting, the moderator said, "I feel God wants to bless this man. Brother Panos, at the close of this meet-

143

ing, you just stand up front here, near the speakers' table, and I want everybody who feels led to do so to come on by and give you an offering."

And that's what happened. I had left Houston in the red. When I returned, I had enough money to pay for my plane ticket, the $700 equity on the house, and the $50 fee to transfer the papers Monday morning.

Earnestine was ecstatic. A bundle of energy, she lit into the tasks of cleaning, packing, and moving.

We hadn't been in our new house a week when we nearly lost it. Earnestine was at the front door, looking anxiously down the street. Chrissy was home already, but Georganna, who went to another school, had not arrived. Earnestine hoped she hadn't gotten lost walking home in the new neighborhood. Suddenly, she heard a loud roaring sound.

"What is that?" she cried. "Chris, come quickly! It sounds like a jet has crash-landed and hasn't cut the motor off."

We went outside. The roaring noise continued. We started to go look for the source of the noise.

"Go back, go back!" a neighbor shouted. "It's the gas main! The gas main has exploded! Get in your car and drive to safety!"

Quickly we got Chrissy and Georganna, who had arrived home minutes after Earnestine heard the noise. We all piled into the car, taking along our next door neighbor and her children. As we drove away, a huge ball of flame erupted into the sky behind us.

"Oh, what will we do?" our neighbor wept. "We'll lose everything."

"No we won't," Earnestine said. "We will pray for God's protection on our houses, and He will hear us." Earnestine and I prayed as I drove the car quickly out of the area. Soon we knew that everything would be all right.

It was about ten in the evening before we were allowed

back into the neighborhood. Our house and our next door neighbor's house were the only two houses on our block that had not sustained damage. Several houses had been totally demolished. The house in front of us looked like the roof had been lifted off and set back crooked. Houses much farther away from the blast than ours had cracked foundations, broken windows, and burned shingles. But not ours. And not our neighbor's. God had kept them safe.

Chapter Nineteen
To Russia, With Love

As I was in prayer one morning, God showed me a picture of a map of Europe. Several cities stood out sharply: Frankfurt, West Berlin, East Berlin, Athens, Istanbul, Vienna, Kiev, Moscow, Odessa, Leningrad, Riga, Tallinn, and Warsaw.

"Pack my bags," I said to Earnestine, "I'm going back behind the iron curtain." I had no money, but I knew that the Lord would supply. It was time to leave again.

I went to the telephone and made reservations. I had wanted a direct flight to Frankfurt, but all I could get was a flight with an overnight stopover in Washington, D.C. The cost was $900.

That evening, I went to Austin, Texas, where I had a speaking engagement. I prayed all the way to Austin, and at the meeting I told the people what God had done in Eastern Germany.

"My heart is heavy and burdened tonight," I told them at the end of my message. "I know God wants me to take the gospel behind the iron curtain once again. The need is very

147

great; my heart aches for the people there. I don't have the money to go yet, but I know that I will go. God will supply the funds I need. Be sure to pray for me."

The love offering totaled less than fifty dollars.

"You're not going anywhere," the devil gibed. "On fifty dollars you're lucky you can get back to Houston. If it had been much less, you might have been stranded here in Austin. You really blew it this time." In the spirit, I rebuked him.

A man and a woman walked up. The man tapped me on the shoulder. I'd never seen either of them before.

"God has given me a vision concerning you," the woman said. "I see you ministering in a strange land. The people are roughly dressed, wearing heavy winter clothing. It is very cold. As you minister, I see guards everywhere. They have machine guns and tanks. I also see barbed wire and vicious dogs. There is a red flag, too, with a hammer and sickle on it."

They turned and left, as quickly as they had come. The devil could lie all he wanted, but I knew God was going to get me where He'd sent me.

People started to file out of the room where I had spoken, many of them stopping to shake my hand and wish me well on my trip. One elderly man asked me, "How much do you need to go to Germany?"

"I think I would need at least $1,000," I said. "The air fare is $900."

"I'll call you in the morning," he said.

I stayed in Austin that night. Early the next morning, the phone rang. It was the elderly man.

"I have been praying all night, and I want to give you $1,000. I sold some land not too long ago, and promised to give the money to missionary work. I think the Lord wants you to have it."

I returned to Houston rejoicing and thanking God.

Before I left, I phoned John and Elizabeth Sherrill, who had just finished writing a book on Brother Andrew, the Bible smuggler. The book had not yet been published, but the Lofferts had told me about Brother Andrew on my last trip to Frankfurt. I got his address from the Sherrills and planned to get in touch with him when I reached Europe. God had other plans. The Sherrills told me that Andrew was on his way to Washington, D.C. Maybe that was why I had been unable to get a direct flight to Frankfurt! I decided to contact him if possible.

God worked it out perfectly. After I landed, I went straight to my hotel. As I walked into the lobby, Brother Andrew walked out of the elevator. We recognized each other immediately, in the spirit. Together, we walked the snowy streets of Washington, D.C. developing a friendship and a liking for each other. Then we went to Andrew's hotel room and spent several hours in prayer. As we prayed, Andrew looked at me.

"Chris," he said, "you will have a ministry in the Communist lands. You are a pioneer, like me, and you will reach many people in the Communist lands.

We thanked God for the open doors He had given us, and for His protection.

I had planned to ask Brother Andrew for contacts behind the iron curtain but, as we prayed, I saw that this was not God's will for me. God Himself would supply my contacts. God did not want me to go to the people that Brother Andrew had already reached; He wanted me to break new ground. I would have to walk in faith.

The following day I left Washington, much encouraged by the time of fellowship with Brother Andrew. As the plane glided over the cold Atlantic waters, I thought about the ministry that God had entrusted to me. As I mused, God showed me that He had chosen me to reach all people, but that I was also uniquely equipped to reach the Orthodox. There are two hundred and fifty million Orthodox Christians in the world who need to be reached by the word of God. The word of God is presented in their churches, but many of them do not realize how to receive and appropriate this word for their own lives. Russians, Romanians, Bulgarians, Greeks, Ethiopians, Indians, Syrians, Armenians, Africans—all belong to Orthodox churches. Many Orthodox live behind the iron curtain.

When we landed in Germany, I went straight to the Lofferts'. I had let them know I was coming, and they had lined up several places for me to preach. In addition, the Lofferts and their pastor gave me heavy winter clothing, including a big, warm overcoat. I arranged to have the overcoat pockets altered so that they extended all the way down to the hem of the coat, and began to pray for gospels of John to fill the pockets with.

I planned to travel over Europe before I entered Russia, but before I went anywhere else, I wanted to make one more trip to East Berlin. There, I fasted and prayed in my hotel room, asking the Lord to supply my traveling expenses and contacts behind the iron curtain. Soon, I was led to go downstairs and break my fast.

From the hotel lobby, I looked outside, and saw two little East German ladies coming down the sidewalk. They looked like they were making a beeline in my direction. Sure enough, they walked straight up to me. Without preamble, one of them said to me, "The same Holy Spirit that is in you is in us." Then, one of them handed me twenty-five dollars in German marks, and the other one gave me ten dollars in German marks and a sack full of fruit. They also gave me a little card with an address on it. The address was in Moscow.

As I held the card in my hand, reading it for a second time, one of the little ladies asked me, "Will you go?" I assured them that I would, and they turned around and made their departure as quickly as they had arrived.

I was amazed. Nobody in East Germany knew that I had been fasting and praying for contacts in Russia—and nobody but the Lord knew that I had been fasting, was ready to break my fast, and liked to break a fast on fruit. Some people may have known that I needed money for my travels, but they were over in West Germany. I had just about run out of money, and my ticket went only as far as Greece, the next stop on my itinerary.

Since the prophecy I'd given the night before the colonels seized power, I'd had an open door in Greece. I spoke there, then hopped over to Istanbul, where I had an audience with the patriarch of the Greek Orthodox church, His Holiness Athenagoras. After I told him my life story, he told me, "Chris Panos, every Greek Orthodox in the world should hear your testimony of how you were saved by God." I held a series of meetings while I was in Istanbul; the patriarch sent a priest along as an observer. In addition to Greek Orthodox, the audience was composed of Turks and Muslims. During the first night's meeting, I felt impressed to stop almost as soon as I started preaching.

"You, there. You with the stick," I said, pointing to a crippled woman in the crowd near where I was standing. "God has healed you. Get up and walk, in Jesus' name."

The woman didn't budge.

"In Jesus' name, walk!" I commanded a second time.

Still, the woman didn't move. *I* knew she was healed, but *she* didn't know it yet. Exasperated, I took the stick away from her, grabbed her arm, and ran her up and down the aisle. Soon, she was running on her own.

The crowds increased, but the Turks were outraged. The following night, before the service, the police arrived.

"You must come with us," they said.

"Why? What have I done?" I asked.

"What have you done? What *haven't* you done? We cannot believe that all these people come here just to hear a sermon. We cannot allow rabble-rousers to come in and stir up trouble."

"Stir up trouble! Believe me, I plan nothing of the kind. Why, you're welcome to come and attend the services and see for yourself. You don't know what you're missing! Last night, a crippled woman was healed by a miracle."

"Yes," said one of the policemen, grimly. "We heard about that 'miracle,' as you call it. We heard you actually took the woman's cane away from her and forced her to run up and down the aisle with you. It was probably all in her head. She probably wasn't really sick at all. You can't call that a miracle!"

"Well, what about the others who were healed?" I asked.

"We heard about that too. You touched every one of them. Who knows what tricks you were up to? We can't have it! You're coming with us!"

"Wait a minute!" I said, seized by an inspiration. "What would you say if people were healed *without* my touching them?"

"Well, then we would have to agree that it was a miracle," they said.

"You just stay here and watch tonight," I told them. "I won't lay hands on the sick, and the miracles will still take place."

"All right," they conceded. "We'll stay and watch. We won't arrest you yet. But you'd better *not* lay hands on the sick. If you so much as touch a single sick person, we'll cart you right off to jail!"

To Russia, With Love

That night I told the people that I had promised not to lay hands on anyone. "But you'll still get healed. I am not the one who does the healing. Jesus does the healing." With that, I turned my attention to my sermon. As I preached, people were healed all through the crowd. It was just like a panorama of the Book of Acts.

The police let me finish out my series of meetings in Istanbul. In obedience to them, I didn't lay hands on the sick for the rest of my stay there. Up till then, I had been praying for the sick one by one at the close of every meeting. After Istanbul, I took to praying one mass prayer for everyone. Instead of diminishing, the number of miracles continued to increase. God had turned a minor harassment into a major blessing, for without this technique of praying for many people simultaneously, I would be unable to hold the mass crusades I hold today. Imagine trying to pray for two hundred thousand people individually! Truly, "all things"—even Turkish policemen—"work together for good to those that love God."

Leaving Istanbul, the next stop was Vienna, where I was just going to spend the night, get my papers straightened out, and then catch a Russian airliner. I was nearly broke. The clerk told me my hotel room would cost twenty dollars a night. I gulped.

"Don't you have anything cheaper?" I asked him.

"Well, we could let you have a maid's room," he responded.

"How much is that?"

"Three dollars a night."

I took it. It was small and sparsely furnished, with no bath, but I was thankful for it. As I began to offer my thanks to God, a strange-sounding syllable kept coming to my mind: Uhl. Uhl. Uhl.

"Uhl? What does that mean?" I prayed. No answer.

I went to sleep and arose the next morning with the syllable repeating in my spirit: Uhl. Uhl. Uhl.

As I was preparing to leave, suddenly I turned to the desk clerk and said, "Uhl." It just popped out. I wondered what I'd said to him.

"Uhl?" he asked. "What is the first name?"

"I'm not sure," I said, knowing what to do now. "Can you just read off the Uhls in the telephone directory? I'll let you know when you come to the right one."

He went to get the directory as I prayed that the Lord would show me which Uhl He was leading me to. The very first name the man read was the Reverend Uhl of the British and American Bible Society. The address listed was just a few blocks away from the hotel.

"That's it!" I said. "Thank you very much."

I was so thrilled I went straight to a telephone and called Reverend Uhl.

"I'm glad you called," he said. "I had a dream last night that a man would be coming here from a foreign country, looking for contacts behind the iron curtain. Come over to my Bible House."

"I'll be there!" I told him.

At the end of my visit with Reverend Uhl, I not only had additional contacts behind the iron curtain, but just as important, I had my overcoat pockets and suitcase full of Russian-language gospels. Now I was truly prepared to enter Russia!

The plane I boarded was making its maiden voyage from Vienna to Kiev. It was a long, thin plane—a converted military aircraft—with two seats along both sides, and none in the middle. It was crude by American standards, but it was headed where I wanted to go—straight into Russia.

When we landed in Kiev, the first thing I spotted was an

enormous picture of Lenin. It dominated the airport, its surface illuminated by enormous floodlights. Guards in uniform were everywhere and the entire airport was covered with snow and ice. I was very thankful for my warm overcoat.

I heard an audible voice. It said, "Chris Panos, you've been preaching the gospel, and you've heard a lot of things and done a lot of things, but let me tell you something. You're not just dealing with ordinary people. These are Russians who have been trained by the KGB. They're able to detect a Bible. And not only are they able to detect a Bible, but they're able to ask you questions. And the way you answer those questions will enable them to detect whether you are for them or against them.

"If you are concealing anything, they'll immediately know. And not only that, but let me tell you something else. By the clothes that you have on, they know where you're from. And even your facial expression will give you away, too. Now I want you just to think about that for a moment. We're not fooling with just some people who don't care whether you bring Bibles into the country or not. They do not love Christianity. Communism is a religion, and it's dead set against Christianity.

"Now," said the voice, "I'm going to give you a solution to this predicament. You see that little washroom?" I saw it. "Well, you just go over to that washroom and hide all those gospels behind the commode. Just get rid of them. Because if you go through customs, they're going to find them. They're going to arrest you. And when they do, you won't be like Peter, Paul, and Silas, praising the Lord in the midst of adversity. Because there's nobody praying for you. Nobody at all."

A cold chill traveled from the crown of my head to the bottom of my feet. Every cell of my skin had a goosebump sitting on it. I was scared stiff! As I stood there frozen, I heard another voice—not audible this time, but from inside of me. And this voice said, "Fear thou not; for I am with thee: be not dismayed; for I am thy God: I will strengthen thee; yea, I will help thee; yea, I will uphold thee with the right hand of my righteousness." I recognized the Scripture: Isaiah 41:10. And then the Lord said, "Son, when you get up to that customs agent, you blind him in the name of Jesus. Do you remember when Barnabas and Saul went over to Cyprus?"

"Yes, Sir."

"You know when Saul blinded the eyes of that sorcerer, Bar-Jesus, for a season, because he saw the subtlety of Satan in him?"

"Yes, Sir."

"Well, blind this man in Jesus' name."

Well, I had Scripture, I had an illustration, and I knew it was the Lord speaking to me this time, because I felt good about it. But I didn't know what was going to happen. It was really hard for me to understand how blinding the customs agent was going to do any good, but I knew I could trust God.

When it came my turn in line, the customs agent looked at me and said, "Which of these is your bag?"

"That one over there," I said. "And I blind you in Jesus' name," I continued, speaking in the spirit.

The agent got my bag and put it on his rack. "Open it up," he said.

"All right." I took it and opened it up, and he looked inside, putting his hand right to the bottom. If you ever carry any gospels into Russia, don't put them on the bottom, put them on the top. I had been led to put them on top. It's better to depend on God. God is smarter than the Russians are! Sure enough, the customs agent didn't notice anything.

Next, he checked another bag of mine. There was nothing in there. Suddenly he looked up and he looked right in my eyes. Again I said, "I blind you in the name of Jesus." Like the last time, I said it in my spirit, not out loud.

Suddenly, the customs agent looked at me and he reached out and grabbed my little brown flight bag. As he did, I heard that first voice again.

"I told you, I told you, I told you," it said. "He's going to find out you've got Bibles in there and he's going to throw you in jail, and you're not going to be able to praise God like Paul and Silas did."

The man unzipped my bag and took out a Bible. He thumbed through it. Then he asked me, "Do you have any other books?"

"Dear Lord, what a question!" I thought. "I have books in every pocket!" And before I knew it, I'd said yes.

When I told the customs agent that I had other books, he looked in the middle compartment and pulled out another Bible. It happened that he was looking at an English Bible, and not one of the Russian gospels, but you'll never convince me he couldn't read the words, "Holy Bible," because he'd read my name and address on my passport very clearly only a moment before.

"Move on," he told me.

I moved on out of customs and into Russia, feeling as though nothing could hold me back. Nothing. I can't explain what it did for me in my spirit, but ever since that moment, I have known that my God can do anything. Anything at all.

Chapter Twenty
The Warsaw Angel

From Kiev, I went on into Moscow, where I checked into the Metropole Hotel. That Sunday, I decided to check out the Russian Baptist Church. Only two churches are permitted to hold services in Moscow: one is the Baptist church and the other is the Orthodox church. Each is permitted to hold services in only one location. Consequently, the Russian Baptist Church has a congregation of 5,000 people. Many of these people, however, do not attend church regularly; it would not be safe for them to visit even this "official" church too often. And much of the congregation is made up of tourists and visitors from out of town.

Services were about to begin as I arrived. A deacon greeted me at the door. "Welcome," he said. "Come and sit with us. We have a marvelous organ and a very good choir. Come sit by us and listen to them." He spoke in English, alerting me to the fact that Russian church officials must be almost as well-trained as the Russian customs agents in the fine art of spotting foreigners.

The Baptist church has a special section for visitors in the balcony, where benches are provided. Down on the main floor of the sanctuary, there are no seats. Here, as in many Greek and Russian churches, it is customary for the congregation to stand throughout the church service. However, I knew that I was not there that morning to listen to a concert of sacred music.

"I am not a tourist," I told the man. "I didn't come here to listen to music. I came to preach the gospel to the people here."

The deacon took me into a back room, which was evidently used as an elders' room. There was a long conference table in it, and several other church officials were back there.

"Do you have any Bibles?" they asked.

"What I have will be available at a later date," I said. "That is not the reason I came here today. God has sent me here with a message for your congregation, and He has sent me here with a message for you."

"We are sorry," one of the men said, "but you cannot preach to our congregation. It is not permitted. We have to be very circumspect and obey all the rules and regulations, or we will not be allowed to hold services at all. But tell us, what is the message that you have for us?"

"The message I have for you is found in the Book of Revelation, chapter 3, verses 15-16. It says: 'I know thy works, that thou art neither cold nor hot: I would thou wert cold or hot. So then because thou art lukewarm, and neither cold nor hot, I will spue thee out of my mouth.'

"The Lord would have you to know that you are lukewarm. You have compromised with the Communists. You are allowed to keep your doors open and hold services only as long as they are not offensive to the party and you tell yourselves that it is better to compromise and continue than to make a stand for Jesus and shut down completely.

"But God's ways are not our ways. That line of reasoning makes sense from a human point of view, but it is not God's way of doing things. What good will it do you if the Russians allow you to operate, and the Lord rejects you? 'And what shall it profit a man if he shall gain the whole world and lose his own soul?'

"That is the message I have for you today. I also have a message for your congregation."

"What do you plan to tell the congregation?" one of the officials asked.

"The plan of salvation," I replied.

"We cannot allow you to preach," he told me. "But we have a ministers' meeting here tomorrow morning. You will be welcome to come and speak to it.

"We can let you speak to the congregation for a moment, but not to preach. Just say hello to them. Bring them greetings on behalf of the people of America. That is always allowed."

And so it was that I spoke to the congregation of the Russian Baptist Church. "I would like to greet you on behalf of the American people," I told them, "who sent me here to tell you that 'God so loved the world, that he gave his only begotten Son, that whosoever believeth in him should not perish, but have everlasting life.' "

As I left the church, one of the elders, a fat man named Orliv, followed me out. He had a cancerous-looking sore on his face. It was ugly, but I somehow wasn't led to pray for him to be healed.

Peering through thick-lensed glasses, Orliv told me, "Coming from America, you wouldn't understand. Here in Russia, we must be very circumspect. We have to be very, very careful. The Russian government has been very good to the Russian Baptist Church. They have even promised to print fifty thousand New Testaments in the Russian language soon. But we wouldn't want to do anything to harm our relationship with the government right now. We cannot afford to rock the boat. Still, if you have any Bibles, we would like to get them. We need Bibles. Few people in our congregation have any."

Orliv followed me all the way back to the Metropole, pleading for Bibles. In the lobby, I told him, "Wait here. I'll be right back." I didn't want Orliv coming up to my room and talking about Bibles. I was sure the rooms were bugged. The Russians, I knew, bug all or most of their hotel rooms. I got about a dozen gospels and brought them back down to him.

"Here," I told him. "Give these to the people who need them most."

Orliv thanked me profusely and left, but somehow I was unable to share his joy. When I got back to the room, the Lord rebuked me. "Chris, you didn't like that fellow, Orliv, did you?"

"No, I didn't," I replied. "He seemed sincere, but I just didn't love him the way I ought to love a brother in the Lord. Maybe it was because of that ugly sore on his face."

"Don't look at the outward appearance," said the Lord. Learn to trust My discernment. Orliv is a compromiser. He is an agent of the KGB. You shouldn't have given those gospels to him. You were not being led to give them to him. Tomorrow morning, you will see them again, and you will know this for yourself."

The following morning, I went to the Baptist church again to speak to the ministers. When I got there, I went straight to the elders' room. I entered just in time to see the gospels I had given Orliv being placed in a safe. The safe was full of Bibles and New Testaments of all descriptions. The man at the safe turned around He looked surprised and a little discomfited to see me standing there.

"Whenever we receive Bibles from our visitors," he said, "we keep them here. We want to make sure that we give them out to the right people."

But the safe was chock full. It couldn't be *that* hard to find the "right people" to give the Bibles to, I thought. Suddenly I knew that the elders had never planned to distribute any of them. Instead, they were destined to be destroyed. I had just seen a dozen of my precious gospels of John go down the drain!

Sobered, I waited till it was time to preach to the elders. When it came my turn to speak, I brought them an expanded version of my message of the day before: the message of the lukewarm church. The memory of the confiscated gospels added force to my delivery as I preached to them.

After preaching to the ministers in the Baptist church, I pushed on into Russia, preaching in the cities God had shown to me on the map He had given me back in Houston. I traveled to Odessa, Leningrad, Riga, and Tallinn, preaching to clusters of people and passing out my remaining gospels. I yearned to help these people. Their hearts were hungry for God and my own heart went out to them.

I was still in Russia when Christmas came. I spent Christmas Day tramping the snowy streets of Moscow, witnessing to everybody I could find. I was far from home that Christmas, but I was not alone, for God was with me. His presence seemed very close that Christmas Day.

Right after Christmas, I went down to the American Express Office in the lobby of the Metropole.

"I'd like to cash this," I told the girl there, handing her a fifty dollar check.

"I will give it to you in rubles," she replied.

"I would prefer American dollars."

"I am sorry, sir, but we are not allowed to give you American dollars, only rubles."

"Well, how about travelers' checks then? American Express Travelers' checks made out in dollars?"

"I don't know. Nobody's ever asked me that before," she answered. "I will have to have somebody check on that."

While we were waiting for the answer, I felt impelled to witness to her.

"What is your name?" I asked her.

"Sonia," she replied.

"Are you an Orthodox Christian?"

"Yes, I am," she replied, looking a little startled. "Why do you ask?"

"I too am Orthodox. But it's a funny thing. Even though I was an altar boy and used to help serve Communion, I didn't understand what the Communion service really meant. Do you know what it means?"

"No, but I would like to know."

Communion is a very special and holy moment in any Orthodox church, and I have found that the Communion service is often the key to witnessing to any Orthodox or Catholic Christian.

"I'll tell what it means," I said. "It commemorates the fact that 'God so loved the world, that he gave his only begotten Son, that whosoever believeth in him should not perish, but have everlasting life.'

"God's Son, Jesus Christ, died on the cross in order to pay the price for our sins.

"When we take Communion, the bread is Christ's body, the body that was nailed to the cross in atonement for our sins, and the wine is his blood, the blood that was shed for us for the remission of our sins.

"Because Jesus Christ paid the price for our sins with His body and with His blood, we do not have to pay the price.

Simply by believing in Jesus, we can have forgiveness for all of our sins. Would you like to have this forgiveness?" I asked.

"Yes, I would," she replied.

Standing right there in the American Express office, my new friend became a new creature in Christ. When she finished, she raised her head. Her face was shining. She had become a child of God. Later, she gave me a gaily-painted wooden spoon for New Year's as a token of her appreciation. The spoon, a traditional Russian design, is a treasured souvenir that now ornaments my office.

In addition to the spoon, Sonia gave me another surprise.

"There is something I must tell you," she said.

"What is that?" I asked.

"I am an agent of the KGB," she said. "All of us are, almost everyone you meet. Everyone who is likely to come in contact with foreigners is trained to spy on those foreigners. But don't worry, I have told them nothing that could harm you."

"Nothing can harm me, Sonia, as long as God protects me. But tell me, why all this spying? What does it accomplish?"

"Oh, many things," Sonia said. "We look for prospective agents among the tourists, and we watch who the tourists contact. We wouldn't want the CIA recruiting Russians to spy on us, as you can imagine!"

"But Sonia," I protested, "what makes you think foreigners would *want* to spy for Russia? Surely most people are loyal to the country that they come from!"

"Oh, they don't *want* to spy on their own countries," Sonia told me, "but they have to. We blackmail them. That is why we need so many agents to learn what weaknesses are available for exploitation. And to collect evidence of those weaknesses. Often we simply file the evidence away. Who knows who will become useful to us ten years in the future?

It's good to have the evidence on hand."

"But Sonia," I protested, "not every foreigner is as decadent as Communist propaganda pictures him. Many
people—even unbelievers—don't go in for such activities."

"Oh, but we can make them," she replied. "We can arrange it so a pretty young Russian girl just happens to fall in
love with one of our visitors, and even provide her with a
husband to catch them in the act. Or, if the person is not
interested in sex, we can often trap him into exchanging
currency on the black market. And if all else fails, we can
fake the evidence."

"Why are you telling me all this?"

"Because I don't want you to get caught."

"But I don't do such things! I am a man of God!"

"Yes. Well, be careful anyway. I do not want you to come
to any harm."

I had a lot to think about after that talk with Sonia. Sonia's
job was recruiting agents for the Communists; mine was
recruiting them for God. And I had recruited her, instead of
the other way around.

February found me in Warsaw, Poland. I shared my testimony with the proprietor of the Bible store on New
Jerusalem Street. He was very excited, and asked me to get
together with some other men. We were to meet in the hotel
lobby. From there, we would go to a place where I would
preach.

"What about an interpreter?" I asked.

"Don't worry," he said, "we will have an interpreter with
us."

I was quite excited as I waited for eight o'clock to arrive.
A handful of men met me in the lobby, but we had difficulty
communicating. The interpreter did not show up.

"Where is the interpreter?" I asked. The Bible store

proprietor spoke some English, but not enough to be able to communicate effectively.

"He did not show up," they said.

"I will not be able to preach tonight. I must have an interpreter. You do not understand enough English, and I understand no Polish at all. Even to talk further with you, I need an interpreter."

Despite the difficulties, we attempted to talk some more, but it was difficult and frustrating. Finally, I looked around and spotted the hotel desk clerk. He had dark brown hair and was immaculately dressed. Because of his occupation, I knew he was bound to be bilingual.

"We need an interpreter," I said. "Can you help us?"

"Certainly," he said. It turned out that he spoke perfect English, although he had a foreign accent which I was not able to place.

Finally, we were able to communicate. I talked with the men. They wanted me to go to a meeting the following night to preach, give my testimony, and tell why I was willing to risk my life to smuggle Bibles into Communist lands; why I was willing to die if necessary to witness to people behind the iron curtain.

Through the interpreter, I thanked the men, who replaced their heavy winter wraps and tramped back out into the frozen streets. I was thrilled but troubled. I felt strange about going. I didn't have a clear witness to speak. Behind the iron curtain, I followed a policy that unless I had a clear witness to do something, I simply wouldn't do it. I turned to thank my interpreter.

"Don't go there tomorrow night," he told me, cutting into my thanks.

"Why not?" I asked.

"They plan to record your words on tape and use them as

evidence against you. If you go, they'll arrest you. They'll throw you in jail and use the tape recording to convict you. I suggest that you get out of Poland immediately. You must not, under any circumstances, meet with those men."

Abruptly, he turned on his heel and walked back behind the desk.

I went back to my room and began to read my Bible and pray, seeking confirmation. Then I began to read my allotted ten chapters for the day. This time, I only got as far as eight, when a verse jumped out at me from my scheduled reading: "Make haste and get thee quickly out of Jerusalem; for they will not receive thy testimony concerning me."

I knew the Lord had spoken. I put down my Bible and went back to the lobby to consult with the desk clerk. He wasn't there.

"Where is the desk clerk?" I asked a bellhop.

"Right over there." He pointed to a fat, blond man.

"No, I want the other one."

"What other one?"

"The dark-haired man."

"I've been here for several years and nobody like that has ever worked for us." The desk clerk told me the same thing.

I went back to my room and packed, convinced that God had sent an angel to warn me to leave the country. I left Poland on the next available flight, and headed home.

Chapter Twenty-One
A Lady Spy Waits in the Dark

I was flying towards Moscow for the umpteenth time. By now, I couldn't remember how many times I'd been in Russia, and even my passport didn't know for sure. The original passport had filled until it looked like a book, and many extensions had been added to it. Finally, they'd had to give me a new one. When the second one was almost full, it had gotten lost. I was now on my third. Leafing absent-mindedly through it, I thought of a conversation with my wife at our home.

"How much time do you think you've spent overseas this year?" she asked.

"I don't know. A lot. Why?"

"Because I've just counted it up, and you've been away for a total of nine months, and only home for three!"

It was true. I'd never been away from Earnestine for more than a couple of months at a time, and sometimes my trips lasted only ten days or two weeks. But although the trips weren't lengthy, they were numerous.

Unable to doze, I spent this flight in prayer, binding the principalities and powers and asking God for contacts, particularly in Moscow University. God had given me a burden to reach the youth of Russia, and Moscow University was, I thought, as good a place to start as any.

As soon as our flight landed, the customs guards herded us towards a big waiting room. There, we watched our luggage being taken from the airplane and wheeled into a separate room. In the spirit, I blinded the customs agents' eyes in the name of Jesus and sat back to wait. And wait.

Two hours passed before the guards returned with the luggage. By then, I was sure that a miracle had already happened. When I had packed, I had placed the gospels and New Testaments I was carrying right on top of everything. The customs agents were sure to have opened my suitcases, yet they had apparently not found them. Eventually, our luggage reappeared and I claimed my bags. Just as I was rejoicing about another escape, one of the agents walked straight up to me. He looked at me for a moment, sizing me up.

"Open that bag," he said, pointing to the larger of my two suitcases.

"In the name of Jesus, I command you not to touch my bags," I replied. Usually, I say such things in the spirit, but this time I spoke out loud. The agent blinked, apparently neither hearing nor understanding the words I'd said. For a moment he stood stock still, looking at me. Then he raised his hand.

"You have waited long enough," he said. "Go on through."

I took my bags and walked away. As I did so, the man went back to the people who were still in line.

"How many of you came in on that airplane?" he asked, motioning towards the Aeroflot jet I'd just arrived on. Almost everybody raised their hands.

"I'll take you one by one," he told them. "Each of you must come by me, so that I can check your bags." The KGB didn't want anyone to know that their bags had already been checked.

I was the only one who had escaped the check.

I traveled on into the center of Moscow and returned to the Metropole again. By this time, I had been fasting and praying for contacts for several days. As usual, my hunger pangs had vanished after the first forty-eight hours or so. Now that the hardest part was over, I planned to continue fasting indefinitely. God had other plans, however. Soon after I reached my room, He said, "Son, go down to the dining room and eat."

I was somewhat surprised, but I obeyed God and went downstairs to the dining room. It was full. Finally, over in the far corner, I saw a single empty table. I threaded my way between the closely ranked tables and sat down.

As I waited for service, I heard many different conversations. Suddenly, I realized that in addition to the buzz of unintelligible Russian voices, I was also hearing snatches of conversation in a language I could understand.

"Greek!" I thought. "Somebody's speaking Greek!" I looked around. At the very next table I spotted the source of the familiar language. Two young Greek girls and a Greek boy who looked to be in his early twenties were holding a spirited conversation.

"*Tikanis*," I greeted them.

"*Tikanis*," they responded.

Still speaking Greek, I introduced myself.

"Sit down! Sit down!" they said. "It's good to hear another Greek voice. Come and eat with us!"

The Greek students introduced themselves as Nikolas, Georgia, and Cleo, Greek students enrolled at Moscow University. I was excited. Perhaps they were to be the contacts

I had prayed for! We chatted back and forth over our food, getting to know one another.

Soon, Nikolas asked me the inevitable question, "What are you doing in Russia?"

I paused and prayed, waiting for God to lead me. He did.

"I smuggle Bibles," I said, slapping a small Russian New Testament onto the marble tabletop.

The three students jerked back as though I had placed a snake on the table instead of the Holy Scriptures.

"Please be careful," they chorused, speaking nearly in unison.

"There are spies everywhere, and they watch very closely," Nikolas explained.

"Don't worry, my God will take care of me." I told them about how I'd gotten through the customs, loaded with gospels and New Testaments. "It was a miracle," I said. "I was the only person on my plane whose luggage wasn't searched."

"We believe in God too," said Nikolas, keeping his voice low. "We are Greek Orthodox. But if I tried such a thing, I am certain I would be arrested. What makes you so bold?"

"I am bold because I know God is with me," I told them. As Greek Orthodox, you already know the way to God, because the Orthodox churches preach the gospel. But it's not enough just to hear the gospel message, you also have to believe it; then you have to act on what you believe. If you do that, then God will do the same things for you as He does for me, as long as you continue to believe that He will.

"Would you like to accept Jesus as your Savior?" I asked Nikolas before we parted.

"Yes, I would," he replied.

"And how about you?" I asked the girls. They looked at each other and nodded.

And there, sitting in the crowded dining room of the elegant Metropole Hotel in Moscow, three Greek students became new babes in Christ. Within a day, they had also become my couriers, smuggling Bibles into Moscow University and distributing them to other students. I had found my contacts, and how beautifully God had worked everything out! In that huge city of six million people, God had led me to the right restaurant in the right hotel—and there, in an enormous and crowded dining room, He had caused me to find a seat less than two feet away from the table at which my prayed-for contacts sat. Not only that, but He had then proceeded to save the contacts, so that they would be willing to take the necessary risks for Him.

That seemed to be my trip for encounters in restaurants. Only a few days after I'd met the Greek students, I entered the Metropole dining room again. This time, it was not so crowded. I found an empty table right away, and sat down.

In Moscow, it is the custom that the first person to sit at a table has the authority to give permission for others to sit down with him or not, as he chooses. As the restaurant gradually filled up, an English couple arrived and asked if they could sit with me.

"Please do," I told them.

British to the core, they ordered tea. It arrived in little glasses encased in silver holders, along with several kinds of pastry. Soon after the tea, a Russian lady came along. "May I sit with you?" she asked in English.

I gave her permission, and she began talking as soon as she was seated. "I teach a class of six-year olds," she informed us. "I tell them of our great father Lenin." She went on to spout a great deal of Communist propaganda about what a great deliverer Lenin was, and how he had delivered Russia from capitalism and from the czar, giving Russia "real freedom." The longer she spoke, the more difficult it was for me to contain myself. It was hard to get a word in edgewise, but she finally had to pause for breath.

"My dear lady," I said, "Lenin was not the deliverer. Jesus Christ is the deliverer of all mankind, including Russia."

"What do you do?" she asked me.

"You are a teacher," I said. "I am also a teacher. I teach that 'God so loved the world, that he gave his only begotten Son, that whosoever believeth in him should not perish, but have everlasting life.' "

I continued to tell her about the shed blood of Jesus Christ and the importance of the Cross. Finally, she could take it no longer. She stood up. "Lenin is the only deliverer!" she said, stamping her foot. Then she whirled around and stalked off.

The rest of us sat in silence for a moment, listening as the enraged staccato of her high heels receded into the background. Then I noticed the young Englishwoman to my right. Her eyes were full of tears.

"If you love this Jesus so much that you would risk everything to tell His story here in Russia, then I want Him to come and live in my heart. I want to receive Jesus Christ as my Savior right now. I want His blood to cleanse my heart."

It was not, I thought, a bad score for one Russian restaurant: three Greek students and one English lady. But the excitement wasn't over yet. Several hours after I led the Englishwoman to the Lord, I headed back to my hotel room.

By American standards, the Metropole Hotel is not luxurious, although the lobby and the dining room retain an old world, high-ceilinged elegance. But in the rooms—at least the rooms I could afford—the furnishings are drab and the comforts minimal. As I went to my room, I brooded about the beds provided by the Metropole: actually, they were little more than small narrow cots. You can imagine my surprise when I opened the door to my room—I was sure it was my room—and found a girl waiting for me on one of those cots. The covers came only just above her waist: from the doorway, I could see that she was wearing nothing but some sort of slip or nightgown.

"Lord," I prayed, "please help me! What shall I do?"

"Tell her about Me."

"You need Jesus," I told the girl, advancing courageously part way into the room. "He died for you. He gave His life for you. He paid for your sins with His blood. 'God so loved the world, that he gave his only begotten Son, that whosoever believeth in him should not perish—' "

With a startled cry, the girl jumped out of bed, grabbed her things, and ran. I stuck my head out into the hallway, intending to watch her retreat, but when I looked, there was no one to be seen. She hadn't had time to reach the elevator or the stairs. Later, I realized that the Aeroflot office was almost directly across the hall from my room. She must have dashed straight out of my room and into the Aeroflot office, which had closed for the day. Possibly, she had even left the door unlocked in case she needed to make just such a strategic retreat.

I did not worry too much about the incident. I had been warned that the KGB was notorious for entrapping foreigners.

It was not long before I had occasion to remember the warnings again. From Moscow, I had traveled on into Warsaw. Poland has lots of beautiful blondes. At that time, however, the Polish people—like most Communists back then—tended to be on the plump side. Their fashions, too, were years behind the times. But the prostitutes were conspicuous by their good looks. Most had blonde hair, slender figures, and wore Western fashions.

"Since you're a Christian," my friend had told me, "I won't

have to tell you to stay away from prostitutes. But you'll be able to spot them easily enough. It's considered unpatriotic to wear Western clothes over there. And prostitution is illegal. Yet the hotel areas are always full of beautiful blonde prostitutes, dressed in the latest Western styles. They get away with it because it's part of their job. They are KGB agents, trained in entrapping foreigners. Western clothes are considered to be just a necessary part of the cover."

The Warsaw hotel was swarming with prostitutes, but I steered clear of them. After a while, the KGB must have decided to try a different approach. I was in the lobby of my hotel when a man came up to me and spoke to me in German. When I failed to respond, he switched to French and then to English.

"Do you want to change your money?" he asked. A black marketeer, he offered me an excellent rate for changing my dollars into zlotys, a rate far better than the going rate at the time. "He is an agent of the KGB," the Holy Spirit whispered. "Lead him to Christ."

"Let's not talk about zlotys," I told him, putting my hand on his arm. "Zlotys and dollars are just small stuff. Let's talk about treasure. Jesus tells us we should lay up our treasures in heaven, 'where neither moth nor rust doth corrupt, and where thieves do not break through nor steal: for where your treasure is, there will your heart be also.' "

Keeping hold of the sleeve of his coat, I continued to witness. Soon I could see that the Holy Spirit was convicting him. Within minutes, I had a new brother in the Lord.

"Now let me ask you something," I said. "You are a KGB agent, aren't you?"

"Yes, I am. How did you know?"

"Oh," I said, "I just knew." I didn't tell him about Sonia or my friend back home, or the fact that the Holy Spirit had informed on him. "As a KGB man, you ought to be able to lead me to some Christian meetings. I haven't had too much success in finding them yet." I told him about my last trip to Warsaw, and the meeting that the Bible store proprietor had planned to tape.

"I know those men," he told me. "They are thick as thieves with the party here. Every one of them is an informer. Your 'desk clerk' gave you the right advice. I will be happy to tell you whom to contact—if you will trust me after that."

"I'm not worried, if you're not," I said.

As good as his word, Peter took me to meet some local Christians. I spoke at several meetings, and Peter translated for me. He introduced me to Catholic priests. I made many contacts for future reference. But soon it was time to leave.

"Let's do one last thing before I go," I said. "Let's go to that Bible House on New Jerusalem Street and get you a Polish Bible."

"But what about the man who owns the place?" Peter asked. "Aren't you afraid he'll trap you in some way? Remember how you left town the last time!"

"Well," I said, "I'm ready to go now, anyway. But I don't think anything will happen. After all, he probably still wants to trap me. By the time he figures out how to do it, I'll have left the country. Or maybe he'll leave well enough alone. Maybe when he sees me with you, he'll figure I'm being trapped already!"

I don't know what the proprietor thought about seeing me again, but nothing happened. I bought Peter a Polish Bible, and then Peter took me shopping for souvenirs. As a going-away gift he bought me several wooden plates and boxes. They were intricately carved and inlaid with delicate designs in metal.

"Thank you," I said. "Every time I look at these, I will think of you. They're beautiful."

At the hotel, we said a sad farewell. The following morning, I left Warsaw for Vienna, where I planned to see Rev. Uhl to replenish my supply of gospels before flying on towards Budapest. I carried with me precious memories, and even more precious addresses. At last, God had opened the doors for me in Poland.

Chapter Twenty-Two
Assignment: Budapest

I was in Budapest, and it was cold. I knew the Lord had a mission for me in Hungary, but what it was I hadn't discovered yet. From the airport, I'd gone straight to my hotel, where I'd checked in and begun to pray. I hadn't been praying long when I got my orders: "Go find a church."

Down in the lobby, I located a bellhop. "Where can I find the nearest church?"

"You must be a foreigner to ask such a question. Don't you know that the church here in Hungary is a fake? You should not waste your time looking for a church. Instead, you ought to give me a great, big tip for saving you all the trouble of looking for one." He held his hand out in the gesture common to bellhops everywhere.

"I want to find a church," I insisted, ignoring his outstretched hand. "There must be one around here somewhere. I went to church in Moscow, and I plan to go to church here as well. Just tell me where it is."

He jerked his thumb over his shoulder. "Back that way.

It's a long walk, but if you just keep on walking down that street, you'll come to it eventually. It's on this side of the street. You can't miss it."

I tipped him and headed for a cab. Soon we were at the church. The dark stone building was locked up tight. The church looked closed, maybe even deserted. I got out of the cab and paid off the driver. As the cab drove off, I noticed a short, pudgy man leaning against the wall of a building near the church. "Walk up to him," God said, "and tell him that the Holy Ghost sent you."

I crossed the street, approached the man, and said, "The Holy Ghost sent me."

"Hallelujah!" the man responded. "My name is Jacob. I have been waiting for you." He took me through a wooden door, along a dimly-lit hallway, through another door, along another passageway and into a room crowded with roughly sixty persons.

"Greetings," said their leader. "I am Brother Pochy. Where are you from?"

"I am from Houston, Texas, in America," I said.

"Hallelujah!" Brother Pochy said. "We have been waiting for you. The Lord told us that a man from the West would be the speaker for this meeting."

For the next hour or so, I spoke to that little gathering of believers as Jacob translated. After the meeting, we had a precious time of fellowship. Jacob, I learned, was a Jew who believed in Jesus. He wanted to go to Israel, but permission had been denied so far. The rest of the men were Plymouth Brethren. They had come from all over Hungary to attend this meeting in Budapest.

"Isn't God's timing perfect?" I asked Brother Pochy. "He led me here to speak just at the time you were having your nationwide meeting."

Brother Pochy laughed. "It is even better than you think.

How did you get to this meeting?"

"God told me to find a church, and when I did, Jacob was waiting and brought me here."

"Well, that's how we all found this meeting. Nobody called this meeting but God. He brought church leaders from all over Hungary here to hear you speak. We would not dare to call a meeting like this. There would surely be at least one informer among the people we invited. If we used the mails, our mail might be read. If we used a telephone, our lines might be tapped. But when God calls a meeting—when He invites the guests—He only calls the people who are meant to be here. At such meetings, we can worship freely. It's a lot better to let God do things His way."

I had to agree with him.

After the meeting, he invited me to come home with him for dinner. There would not be much, he warned, but he wanted a chance to talk some more. Jacob came along to translate.

As we walked the blocks to Brother Pochy's house, I shivered with cold despite my winter coat, but he seemed immune to it. He wore his coat over his shoulders, not even bothering to put his arms in the sleeves. Jacob, however, kept his coat firmly buttoned. Our breath made little clouds in front of our faces and ice crunched underfoot as we walked. Suddenly, God said to me, "Expect a miracle." I was excited. As far as I was concerned, I had just seen a miracle. If God was going to do something even greater, He was about to do something really special.

After a fifteen or twenty minute walk we arrived at a dingy, four-story building. Pale yellow light shone dimly through the sooty grime on the windows, signaling that many of its residents were at home. If it hadn't been for the lights, I would have guessed that the building was as empty as the church had been. It looked bleak and forlorn. Our breath made little puffs of vapor in the unheated air of the stairwell as we climbed to the top floor, where Brother Pochy lived. When we reached the landing in front of his door, we paused.

"I don't know what it means," I said, "but God told me to expect a miracle."

Jacob translated.

"We need a miracle so bad—we need a miracle," Brother Pochy whispered. "Oh, thank you, Father!" He pushed the door open.

The door swung aside to reveal a single room, with a worn gray carpet covering the floor. It was so old that most of the pile had worn away, leaving only the bare, once-white ribs of the weaving to cover the floor. In the middle of this rug stood a huge wooden rocking chair. A slender teen-age girl sat in the chair with a tray of food on her lap. Although the room was cold, she wore only a slip. Her hair was tangled and matted and fell in snarls around her shoulders. Her face was dirty. As we walked in, the girl screamed and screamed. It required no gift of discernment to know that she was possessed by demons. The screams were long and horrible. They sounded like they came from the very pit of hell.

As the girl screamed, she grasped the tray on her lap and threw it at Brother Pochy's head. She missed. The metal tray crashed against the wall, splattering food across the faded paper. The bowl that had contained the food hit the floor and shattered. She stopped screaming. Nobody said anything; the silence was almost as eerie as the screaming had been. Then she started to scream again, this time voicing not shrieks but words I was sure were obscenities. Jacob didn't translate. She tore at her slip and scratched her shoulders with long, ragged fingernails.

"In the name of Jesus Christ, I command you to shut up," I

said in English. "I command you to obey the resurrected power of Jesus Christ."

The girl stopped screaming before Jacob had time to translate. Although the girl understood no English, the devils evidently understood either the words or the authority behind them. In any case they are always forced to submit to the name of Jesus, in any language.

"Come out of her," I said to the devils, "in the name of Jesus Christ."

I worked with the girl for a long time. In the end, seventy-two demons were cast out: lust, greed, envy, jealousy, hatred, murder—on and on they came, naming themselves as they fled.

Indoctrinated by the Communists, the girl had not believed in the existence of God. As the last demon left, she was born again, without any preaching or prompting. She had felt the power of God. Now she knew His reality. No longer did she hate and resent her father. Brother Pochy and his daughter had a tearful reunion and reconciliation, sobbing and hugging each other as Jacob and I smiled through our tears.

Chapter Twenty-Three
One Diamond Towards Red China

"Go to Red China."

"But Lord, You know Red China is closed to Americans!"

"Go to Red China."

There are no closed doors to God, but all the same, in 1968 it was hard to understand why God was telling me to go to Red China. Back then, it was illegal for an American citizen to enter that country. If he did go, he was on his own. The American government would take no steps to protect his rights.

The U.S. government is a great world power, but I planned to go under the protection of a higher power yet. On this journey, I would be representing the kingdom of heaven.

I began fasting and praying, asking God for a financial miracle as confirmation of what He had told me to do. During this time, I shared my plans with the members of a prayer meeting in Shreveport, Louisiana.

"I don't know how and I don't know when, but I'm going to

Red China. I don't know what I'll use for money, or how I'll get the necessary visas, but I'm going somehow. God has sent me."

The prayer meeting was held in an old, two-story house. The power of God fell. People were saved and healed. Signs, wonders, and miracles were poured out upon the gathering. It was just like the overseas crusades.

When we were through, a young woman approached me. "Brother Panos," she began hesitantly, "are you really going to Red China?"

"Yes," I said, "I really am."

She handed me a diamond ring. "God told me to give you this. Use it to pay your way."

I was overwhelmed. "I don't know how to thank you. I don't know what to say." The ring was beautiful. I held it between my thumb and index finger and watched the fire in the heart of the gem.

"I wouldn't give it to you unless God had spoken to me," she said. "It is very dear to me. The ring has been a prized possession in our family for several generations."

"This is a great blessing," I said. "God has used you, not only to provide money for traveling expenses, but also to confirm His will to me."

Inwardly, I praised the Lord. "Thank you, Lord—thank you. I know you have confirmed your will to me—thank you." In addition to the ring, I also received an offering of fifty dollars, which was enough to pay my expenses. From Shreveport, I planned to go to Amarillo and Midland, Texas, for other meetings, and the cash would help me get there.

In Midland, God moved in power. The presence of God was electrifying. Again, many were saved and healed. The following morning, I met a woman who had been in the meeting the night before. Without a word, she walked up to me, handed me a check for $500 and left. I never even got a chance to thank her.

God was providing, but I still had the ring. As I prayed about what to do with it, God told me to call a friend in Beaumont. I didn't want to do it.

"He'll think I'm just after money," I said to the Lord.

"Call him anyway," the Lord said.

"I'd like to come see you," I told my friend. Suddenly, I had peace. I knew the Lord would prepare his heart for what I had to ask him.

Later that day, I flew to Houston. Immediately, I got my car and drove down to Beaumont.

"I don't know anyone who wants to buy a diamond, Chris," he said, "but as long as you're here, let's have a prayer meeting. Why waste a trip?"

We called a quick prayer meeting, and again God moved in power. As I preached, God seemed to point out one of the men to me. Somehow I knew he was connected with selling the diamond.

"Sir, please don't misunderstand me, but I think God has told me to speak to you about this matter. I have been given a diamond ring to use to spread the gospel. God has shown me that you will help me sell it."

"Oh, Brother Panos, I wish you had come a day earlier," he said. "Just today, I bought my wife a new diamond ring."

I showed him the ring.

"That is beautiful, he said. "Say, wait a minute! My business partner is interested in a ring for his wife. He has been looking around. Let me take this with me. I will show it to him and call you in the morning."

He took the ring and put it in his pocket. Never let a stranger wander off with a diamond ring of yours, unless you have God's leading. In the natural, it would have been a foolhardy thing to do, but since God had pointed the man out to me in the first place, I didn't lose any sleep over it.

I lost my sleep over something else instead. The devil kept me awake that night, playing his old familiar tune. "You're crazy," he said. "You've come up with some stupid stuff in the past, but this really takes the cake. What do you think you're going to do in Red China? They'll kill you. Or else they'll arrest you and put you in jail, and when they do, you won't be able to praise God like Paul and Silas did."

By now I'd heard the devil's message so many times he was beginning to sound like a broken record.

"In Jesus' name," I said, interrupting him, "shut up!"

Instant peace. My heart was flooded with assurance. It wasn't my time to die. Suddenly, I remembered that God had appointed me to proclaim His Son before the second coming. I was sure my task wasn't finished yet. Nothing could touch me until it was.

In the morning, the phone rang. It was the man from the prayer meeting. His partner was offering a good price for the ring. Should he sell it? I told him to go ahead. He delivered the money later that day.

A few days later, I went to the Air France office in Houston. The ticket agent was a lovely blonde woman named Cynthia Parker.

"May I help you?" she asked.

"I want to go to Red China," I announced. There was a long silence, as she looked at me.

"I will send a Telex for you," she said finally. "I'll do what I can." She promised to phone me when the arrangements were made.

I was out of town for the next few days, preaching in meetings across Texas. When I got home again, Earnestine handed me a pile of phone messages. Several of them were from Mrs. Parker. I called Air France.

When Mrs. Parker heard my voice, she began to weep. "I must see you," she sobbed. "I must see you quickly."

"Lord, what shall I do?" I prayed.

"Go see her," He answered.

I promised to meet Mrs. Parker in the lobby of a nearby hotel in half an hour. When I entered the lobby, she burst into tears a second time. Through the tears, she told me that she was a backslider. She and her husband had been good Christians when they married but they had become lukewarm. Then, somehow, they had drifted away from God. Now, she had repented.

I rejoiced, and waited. In my spirit, I sensed that there was more than that. There was.

"Don't go to Red China," she blurted. "Please don't think I am crazy, but don't go to Red China. They are going to kill you. After you left the office the other day, a strange thing happened. I saw you on a cross with blood dripping from your hands and face. There were spikes driven through your hands. Please don't go to Red China. They are going to crucify you like they did Christ. Please, please, please don't go!" She buried her face in her hands and sobbed.

"Don't worry," I told her. "Please don't worry. God told me to go. He confirmed His word several times. It would be a great honor to die for Christ, but don't worry. I am sure it just is not my time yet. Who knows? Maybe some day I will be crucified in China. I don't know what your vision means, but it doesn't matter. The important thing is that God used it to draw you back to Him."

Her fears somewhat assuaged, Mrs. Parker agreed to help.

As word of my intentions spread, I began to receive messages from across the nation that people and prayer groups and churches were fasting and praying for me. Many people told me that they had once thought of Red China as closed to the gospel. When they heard my plans, many began to intercede for that nation.

189

God was doing a work in people's hearts, and I hadn't even left the country yet. Mrs. Parker wasn't sure I'd ever get to leave. She had applied for a visa through Hong Kong, Cambodia, France, Pakistan, everywhere she could think of. The U.S. government heard about my plans. An official wrote and warned me that if I entered Red China, I would be on my own. Should the Communists detain me for any reason, the U.S. government would not intervene. He strongly advised that I abandon my plans.

About this time, I began to suspect that the CIA was tapping my phone. My suspicions proved to be correct. After all, they must have reasoned, anyone who wants to visit China might easily be subversive. I didn't mind the tap at all. I just preached a little harder whenever callers phoned for counsel. Every preacher likes a captive audience.

As far as the visa went, all doors remained tightly closed. Mrs. Parker ran out of ideas. Finally, I decided to fly to Hong Kong and work out the details myself, with the Lord's help. Air France made the arrangements. It was to be a direct flight, except for one brief stop in Tokyo.

As my plane approached Tokyo, I had a vision. I don't ordinarily have a lot of visions, but I had one that day. It was extremely vivid. In it, I was walking down a street on the Kowloon side of Hong Kong. (Kowloon is Hong Kong's mainland district; Victoria is the part that is actually on Hong Kong Island.) In my vision, I was not far from the railroad station from which trains leave en route to Canton. As I walked, I saw my friends, Mr. and Mrs. Glenn Ewing. With them was their daughter Edna, Jack Locker's wife.

In Tokyo, I bought a postcard and hastily scrawled a brief note about the vision to Earnestine before boarding my plane for Hong Kong.

On the jetliner, I spent my time gazing out the window, admiring the shining vista of sky and sea. Soon the massive mountains of mainland China loomed in the distance. When we approached the British Crown Colony for a landing, the sight was so beautiful that it took my breath away: hilly, deep green islands set in the shimmering, junk-studded blue of the South China Sea. In the harbor, small craft of all descriptions sailed side by side with huge, ocean-going vessels. I was fascinated. I wondered which of the mountains I'd glimpsed were located in Communist territory. It was a beautiful day, and all seemed right with the world. But just in case, I bound the powers, principalities, rulers of darkness, and wicked spirits.

I checked into the President Hotel in Hong Kong and fell into bed, exhausted by a combination of jet lag and excitement. The next morning, I woke early and went looking for the China Travel Service. I found it on the second floor of an old building. I reached the top of the stairs to find a largish room, jammed with people. There was nothing to do but get in line. While I waited, I noticed that signs in several languages covered the walls. Those in English were filled with charges and slogans directed against the United States. Those in other languages were probably the same. Pictures of Mao were everywhere. So were his little red books—the *Sayings of Chairman Mao* that are even, I regret to say, sold in many U.S. bookstores. Finally, my turn came. The man in the blue "people's uniform" took my application for a visa without comment. I was sure that I would get it. After all, "with God, nothing shall be impossible."

On my way back to the hotel, I strolled along the crowded streets, looking at the incredible array of merchandise being offered for sale by shops and street vendors and dodging the even more incredible traffic. Finally, I decided it was time to return to my hotel. I was nearly there when I had my vision again. There were Mr. and Mrs. Ewing, accompanied by their daughter Edna.

191

"Hey, Brother Ewing," I shouted. I just couldn't help it, it had seemed so real. The man in the vision turned and froze, grasping his wife's arm.

"Look, it's Chris Panos," Edna said.

I ran across the street. It wasn't a vision after all; this time it was real, the fulfillment of what I had seen on the plane. I told them about the vision and we all rejoiced at the wonderful workings of God. We stopped for soft drinks and spent the afternoon like tourists, riding the Star Ferry between Hong Kong's Kowloon and Victoria districts and crawling up to the top of Victoria Peak in a tram that travels at a horrifying forty-five degree angle. From the top, we looked down at the skyscrapers of Victoria separated from the mainland by a spectacular junk-studded crescent of the South China Sea. In the distance was Kowloon, and behind it the mountains of mainland China. The view was breathtaking.

Finally, exhausted, we called it a day. "Isn't God wonderful?" I asked. "He brought you all the way from Waco, Texas, and me all the way from Houston, just to have us meet in Hong Kong, on the other side of the world!"

Before bed that night, I prayed for guidance.

"My son," the Lord said, "because of your constant bold petition to open Red China, I will open it up to you, and when you go to China it will touch thousands of lives in America and around the world. People everywhere will believe that there are no closed doors to the gospel. Already, just through your decision to go, people have caught a new vision. Before, China looked so inaccessible that many weren't even praying about it. Now, they are praying. Soon, groups of businessmen, and even an American president, will visit China. China will be opened up.

"I am pleased with your obedience in coming on this journey. One day you will surely preach to great crowds in

Peking. But do not be surprised. Soon I am going to redirect your path."

Suddenly, I felt wide awake. I no longer wanted to go to bed. Instead, I got dressed and went out into the cool night air. I walked the neon-lit streets of Hong Kong and praised the Lord.

The following morning I was on my way to take the Star Ferry to the Victoria side on Hong Kong Island. As I passed the YMCA Hotel where Brother Ewing was staying, God said, "Go see Brother Ewing."

As I went into the old hotel, I received another impression: "Go into the chapel." There I found Brother Ewing, deep in prayer. When he finished, we went out for tea at the beautiful Peninsula Hotel, admiring the lobby with its hundred chandeliers and stately columns on our way to the dining room. As we seated ourselves at the table, Brother Ewing told me what was on his heart.

"Chris," he said, "you must not go to Red China. You will get your visa, but you are not to go. I heard the audible voice of God give me this message for you. God also told me to tell you this: your timing is right, but conditions are not right yet. Thousands of people will be killed and the leadership of Red China will be shaken up."

We talked about God's message. Brother Ewing thought Mao would probably be assassinated, but when the words of God came to pass, it was actually Lin Pao not Mao, who was killed.

I received my visa, but did not go, obeying what God had told me. A few days later, there was a huge disturbance at the Canton train station, about the time I would have arrived had I gone. Several hundred Chinese were killed in the melee. In spite of this, I wondered why God had brought me all the way around the world, only to tell me not to enter Red China at this time.

Questions raced through my mind. Hadn't God known when He sent me here what would happen in Canton? Had I missed my leading? What would that girl think, the one who had given her ring so that Red China could be reached? Would she have sacrificed her ring if she had known that at the end of the trip I'd be no closer to the Red Chinese than before?

I couldn't help being disappointed as I started to make arrangements to fly back to the United States.

As I brooded about not being able to enter Canton, I wondered what Brother Ewing had meant when he said, "Your timing is right, but conditions are not right yet." How could my timing be right? If my timing were right, I reasoned, surely God would have allowed me to go. Surely He could have stopped an uprising or two if it had suited His purposes!

Suddenly I became aware that God had something to say to me.

"Son," He seemed to be asking, "if you were to get into Red China, what would you take them? How would you get My word to them?"

I had no answer. The last time I had seen Brother Andrew, he had told me about his own experiences behind the bamboo curtain. He and his helpers had smuggled in some New Testaments in a Chinese dialect, but had been unable to give them away. There are more than 200 dialects in China, and nobody they had approached had been able to read this version.

Language had always been a problem in China because there never was a universal language for the whole country. Recently, however Mao's cultural revolution had done what had never been done before in the history of China. First, Mao introduced a single, unified language called New Chinese. The cultural revolution caused such upheaval in previously isolated population groups that New Chinese became the only practical method of communication. **Never before since the birth of Christ has China had one intelligible language all over that vast nation.**

Suddenly, I realized that God wanted me to bring His word to the Communists in a language called New Chinese. Brother Andrew had told me that there were no **New Chinese Bibles or New Testaments available.** That was all right: I would have some printed. This was my mission in Hong Kong! This was why I was here. This was why God had said my timing was right. It takes time to translate and print new Bibles. By the next trip though, or the one after that, I would have something to take with me as I entered Red China. And meanwhile, I had learned a little more about the leading of the Holy Spirit.

As I prayed about the Bibles, God showed me that whole Bibles would take too long to translate. They would be expensive and bulky to carry. For now, we would print New Testaments. And we would print them to look like *The Sayings of Chairman Mao*, the little red book that the Chinese Communists carry with them wherever they go. The same size and shape, covered in the same shade of red, our New Testaments would be wearing the perfect disguise! Lord willing, our Chinese brothers could even be seen reading them and, barring a close inspection of their reading material, they would not get caught.

I contacted others in Hong Kong who shared a burden for the Chinese, and we formed an organization to print the New Testaments. We called it the China Bible Fund.

Since then, I have been in Red China several times, distributing New Testaments and winning people to Jesus Christ. Red China is a whole new ball game, much more dangerous and difficult even than Russia. Many of the Chinese Christians have been terribly persecuted by the Communists.

I remember one white-haired old man. He was beautiful—dignified and well-dressed. He had just been released from prison. The secret police had told him that if he would not preach about salvation and the second coming of Jesus Christ they would not bother him further.

His brothers and sisters in Christ asked him, "Why don't you just retire now and let the younger saints win souls? Do as they say; you have paid a great price already. You have been in prison dozens of times for the gospel. We love you and don't want you to suffer any more."

To me it seemed as though the glory of God permeated even the atmosphere around this man. In my spirit, I could see a light shining around his whole body. He answered them joyfully. "Brothers and sisters, you see I count it a privilege to suffer just a little for the sake of the gospel. I am not only willing to be beaten, but I am willing to die."

When he turned his head, I saw that this beautiful face had been marred by a hot branding iron. Both hands had been tortured. I was later told that the Communists had pulled off all his nails, one by one. Then, some of his fingers had been amputated. This is the man who said, "I count it a privilege to suffer *a little* for the sake of the gospel!"

According to the Book of Acts, the early Christians won three thousand souls in one day. If we were to have a revival like that in Red China, it would take us 725 years to reach the nation. The population of China increases by fifty-five thousand every single day. If we were to print one tract for every Chinese living now, the cost of printing alone would come to something over twenty-one million dollars. Eight hundred million people live in Red China, and most of them have never heard the name of Jesus Christ.

In China, as in any other country, I believe God has showed me that the nationals are the answer. We must teach Chinese to reach Chinese. In the end, Red China will be evangelized by the Chinese themselves.

Chapter Twenty-Four
Around the World on Fifty Dollars

I hadn't been home from China very long when I was raring to go again. I was restless. I couldn't eat; I couldn't sleep. I know it sounds dramatic, but the urge to preach was burning like fire in my bones. It was all I could do just to sit still. I counted up my resources: after cutting our household budget to the limit, I had fifty dollars left. That wasn't even enough to get me off the ground.

The trip I envisioned would be the longest I had ever taken. I wanted to combine many trips into one and travel around the world preaching the gospel. It made sense, I thought, to do it that way. It would conserve the Lord's money, for one thing.

My usual procedure was to fly from Houston to my destination, preach in several different cities or countries, and then fly back to Houston. But I have to admit that that wasn't my primary motive. My real desire was a longing to take the Great Commission literally, to "Go . . . into all the world and preach the gospel."

I was convinced that the Lord wanted me to take the trip,

but although I prayed again and again, no money came in.

"Lord, what's holding up the money?" I prayed. "I know you want me to go. When are you going to supply the funds?"

"My grace is sufficient for thee," He answered.

I tried again. "Lord, fifty dollars isn't even enough to get me out of the country, much less around the world. What am I going to do? I know you gave me this zeal to go, and you know how much I want to get started. I know you're going to send me the money, too, because your word says you will supply all my needs. But Lord, I want it now."

"My grace is sufficient for thee," He answered.

That troubled me. I know that Paul prayed three times for deliverance from a messenger of Satan. Each time, the Lord answered Paul by saying, "My grace is sufficient for thee: for my strength is made perfect in weakness." If the Lord was telling me His grace was sufficient for me, this might be one time I wasn't going to get the finances I had prayed for. Again and again I prayed. Again and again God answered the same way. Finally, I began to realize that God was telling me to go around the world anyway, without the finances I was asking for. He wanted to see if I would trust Him to supply my needs as they appeared.

I got ready to go. My total resources still added up to only fifty dollars.

I charged the airline tickets, praying that God would give me the money for them when the bills came due. The tickets cost thousands of dollars. Earnestine was troubled. It was one thing to sell everything and go and preach the gospel, but it was another thing to go into debt to do it.

My wife was worried, but my friends were horrified. Even the most consecrated of my Christian friends thought I'd really gone overboard this time. Putting it as tactfully as he knew how, one of my best friends protested over the telephone. "You've gone crazy, Chris," he said.

My friends and acquaintances seemed to have divided themselves into two camps, those who thought I was insane, and those who thought I was presuming on God. Shaken by their reaction, I sought God again and again as my departure date neared. The old "religious question" had reared its head, the question Satan asked Eve in the garden of Eden: "*Hath* God said?"

"Lord, is this really you?" I prayed. "Do you really want me to go with only fifty dollars in my pocket? Am I hearing right, Father, or am I really presuming on you?"

Again and again, all that God said was, "My grace is sufficient for thee." Finally, I knew that I was to go, taking only the fifty dollars.

It was a crisp fall morning when Earnestine drove me to Houston's International Airport. After we said goodbye, I boarded a jet for Paris. The flight took all day, and we landed at Orly Airport in the early hours of the morning. There, I learned that my connecting flight had been canceled. The airline provided a limousine to the hotel. When I asked the hotel desk clerk if he had a room available, he answered, "Yes, sir. That will be twenty-five dollars."

Twenty-five dollars! I felt sick. I was planning to go around the world on fifty dollars, and now half of it was to evaporate on my very first night in Paris. There wasn't much I could do about it, though, so I took the room.

It was early morning, and I had only three or four hours in which to sleep, but the thought of losing half my money for that short time drove all thought of sleep away. As soon as I was alone in my room, I dropped to my knees and began to pray. The devil was trying to steal my money—and my faith.

I cried out to God. "Am I in your will, Father? Am I doing the right thing? Is this really faith? Or is it foolishness like everybody said?"

As I poured out my heart to God, my Bible fell open. I turned to my daily reading. As I did, a verse seemed to leap from the page: "Now therefore, I pray thee, if I have found grace in thy sight, shew me now thy way . . ." (Exodus 33:13).

"Show me now, Lord," I prayed. "Show me now. I want to know for sure. I believe I am in your will. Prove it, Lord. You know the hotel bill is twenty-five dollars. You know how much it takes every month to take care of my family back in Texas. Oh, Lord, show me now."

The presence of God flooded that hotel room, and my eyes fell on the next verse. "My presence shall go with thee, and I will give thee rest."

Hallelujah! Instantly, I was full of boldness, faith, and power. Only God's impartation of faith can change a fearful, doubting skeptic into a man of faith. The Bible tells us that we accomplish things "not by might, nor by power, but by my spirit, saith the Lord of hosts." And it is not by might, nor by willpower, but by God's Spirit that we become useful to God. I arose from my knees a new man. Moments before, I'd felt like turning and running back to Houston. Now, I was ready to march to my death if He asked me to. God was with me!

When I finished praying, the sun was just beginning to rise. The bedspread was wet with my tears, but I was full of joy. I knew that I had overcome. I went downstairs and had breakfast, untroubled now by the prospect of spending half my money for one night's lodging. I knew God would supply whatever else I needed.

When I checked out, I found that Satan hadn't been able to take my money, after all.

"Mr. Panos," the desk clerk told me, "we made an error. The airline picked up the tab. There's no need for you to pay."

The airline's limousine picked me up at the hotel and took me back to Orly Airport, where I boarded a plane for Athens. In Athens, I checked into the Electra Hotel, which I planned to make my base of operations for the next phase of my trip.

Because of my prophecy of the colonels' taking power, I had an open door in Athens. I spoke in some of the small churches there. Then, accompanied by two Greek Christians, I headed by car for Albania.

Of all the Communist countries I have visited, Albania and Red China are the two most tightly closed to the spread of the gospel. This is no coincidence. Albania's national leader, Enver Hodscha, patterns himself after Mao Tse Tung. When China had a cultural revolution, part of which involved even greater repression of any traces of religion, Albania had one too. It was in the first flush of Albania's cultural revolution that I entered that country. I brought no Bibles with me. There were none to bring. Since the revolution, the Communists have been developing a unified Albanian language to replace the three different dialects—Gheg, Skchip, and Tosk—that are native to Albania. But although the American Bible Society has one copy of an 1824 Skchip New Testament, none of the Bible societies had, at least at the time I inquired, any Bibles in the new Albanian language. So I entered Albania with only a small handful of tracts.

When our car crossed the border, the customs officials told us that we would have to report to a central office downtown in order to present our passports again and receive a guide, who would function as our interpreter. In Communist countries, these government-supplied "guides" invariably double as spies.

"How many languages do you speak?" the officials asked when I arrived.

"Two," I answered, "English and Greek."

The paperwork was over with quickly, but it took about twenty minutes for our interpreter to show up.

"Are you Mr. Panos?" he asked when he arrived.

"Yes," I said, suddenly aware that he had spoken—and I had answered—in Greek.

"I am Gus" he said, still speaking in Greek.

Hallelujah! My spirit rejoiced. If there's anything I like, it's a chance to witness to someone who was born Greek Orthodox. Sure enough, Gus was. Although born in Albania, he had had a good Greek Orthodox upbringing before he had turned from the church to join the Communist party. As the day progressed, we got to know one another better. Soon the Lord whispered, "Tell him your testimony."

I told Gus the story of my life. Beginning with my Greek Orthodox childhood, I told him about my love for the Greek Orthodox church and the way that God had touched me in the hospital. By the end of the afternoon, Gus had beautifully received Jesus Christ as his Lord and Savior.

"Mr. Panos," Gus said, "when I prayed that prayer with you, I felt Jesus coming in! I feel Him in here!" Excitedly, he stabbed one stubby forefinger at his chest.

Gus bubbled over with joy for a few hours as he took me sightseeing. Soon he grew pensive. I bided my time, praying silently. I could not ask a man to risk his life to spread the gospel. Only God could do that. From the struggle I saw reflected on Gus's face, I thought that perhaps that was just exactly what God was doing. Finally, Gus broached the subject on both our hearts.

"Mr. Panos," Gus said, "to be a Christian in this country is very difficult. Since the cultural revolution, the penalties are very severe. When they catch someone, they interrogate him unmercifully in order to get him to talk. One man I know of was beaten on the bottoms of his feet. That's all they touched. But they beat him until his tongue had swollen with the pain.

"And worse than the torture, I think, is the constant fear. Every Albanian lives with the knowledge that no one can be trusted, no one at all. For here we have the Hidden Brother system."

"Hidden Brother?" I asked. "What's that?"

"A Hidden Brother is an informer. Somewhere in every group of workers—on every city block—in every apartment house—there is a Hidden Brother. He is paid to report on all those who disobey party orders, on those who are not enthusiastic about the party, on those who do not have an approved attitude. And he always does what he is supposed to do; he never looks the other way. Because he knows that somewhere else in the group that he has been assigned to spy on, there is another Hidden Brother whose job it is to spy on him."

"That must be very hard to live with," I said.

"Hard? It is nearly unbearable! And now that I have accepted Jesus, it will be even harder. Because now I know that this system is part of a conspiracy aimed at keeping my people from coming to know their God. Now that I know that God is real, I feel that I must help. You must tell others what you have told me. I will see what I can do."

In the days that followed, Gus led me to various Greek Orthodox officials in Albania. They, in turn, led me to other Christians. Gus translated as I preached. God had beautifully and sovereignly opened a door in one of the hardest Communist nations.

I found out just how difficult Albania was on the few occasions when I ventured out without Gus. It proved impossible to give away the small supply of tracts I had brought along with me. Whenever I would hold out a tract, the well-trained Albanians would simply put both hands behind their backs, instead of reaching out to take it. Finally, I left two small piles of tracts in a couple of strategic places: in the men's room of my hotel, and on a park bench, weighted down with a small piece of rock. Several days later, I checked my deposits. Not a single tract had been taken. Sadly, I gathered them up again. I didn't want some innocent Albanian to be blamed for my evangelistic efforts.

From Albania, I went back to Athens and checked into the Electra Hotel again. There, I sent a Telex to my wife to let her know I was all right. When I had made the reservations for this trip, Cynthia Parker had put a VIP notation on my ticket. Back then, Air France agents were allowed to send Telexes free of charge to their VIP customers. Even money could be Telexed to them, although there was a limit of $200 per city. I was hoping to receive $200 by Telex as soon as Earnestine learned that I was back in Athens, but no money materialized. There was a stack of mail waiting for me at the Electra, but it contained only a few small donations.

In the back of my mind, I began to consider using my "ace in the hole." When I sold everything and went to preach the gospel, I had retained my American Express credit card. If I got in a bad enough jam, I thought, I could always use it. After I had been at the Electra for about ten days, it looked like the jam was on me.

"Mr. Panos," the desk clerk informed me, "you've run up quite a bill by now. Would you be kind enough to settle the balance so far?"

Kind enough I was, but rich enough I wasn't. "I'll settle it tomorrow," I said. "I have to visit American Express first."

I thought about paying the bill by using my American Express card at the hotel. But instead, I decided to write a check for fifty dollars, which would give me some change left over. I planned to Telex Earnestine to take care of the check back home. When I got to the office, I handed the girl the check and my credit card.

"I'm sorry, sir, I can't cash this," she said. "Your card has expired." Sure enough, it had. Now, instead of trusting in American Express, I was going to have to trust in God. Chagrined, I had a sneaking suspicion that that's what He'd been after all along.

From the American Express office, I went straight to my hotel room and sought the Lord. You talk about praying! I probably haven't ever prayed for finances as hard as I prayed back then.

"Lord, you said you were with me. You said you would supply all my needs 'according to your riches in glory.' Lord, I could use some of those riches now. You know I need to pay my hotel bill. Lord, you've got to help me!"

I spent the afternoon praying, and in the evening, I went to a little Greek church to give my testimony. They took up a collection afterwards, but I didn't expect much from it. There had only been about a hundred people in the congregation, and most of them looked poor. During the service, they took up an offering. Later, one of the elders handed me an envelope.

"We were touched by your testimony of how you preached the gospel in Russia," he said. "You are doing a good work. We cannot go ourselves, but this is to help you go. This, at least, we can do."

Later, when I looked in the envelope, I found thirty thousand drachmas—roughly one thousand dollars. I was stunned. After I paid my hotel bill, I still had more money left than you were allowed to take out of the country at that time. In addition, the following day I received $200 from Earnestine by Telex.

"Lord, give me favor with the officials," I prayed. "Work a

miracle so I can take this money with me."

I went to the Bank of Greece and told them what I wanted.

"We are very sorry, Mr. Panos, but we cannot do that. It is not allowed. We can let you take the legal limit with you, but no more."

"I am not a businessman," I said. "I am a minister. I am not taking this money out of Greece to invest it in a business somewhere else. I am taking it to supply my needs as I take the gospel into all the world.

"I am of Greek extraction, and this is Greek money. It was given to me because I told the congregation how I preach the gospel behind the iron curtain, in Russia. That is God's calling on Greece. It was from Greece that the spread of the gospel began in the days of the early Church fathers, and it is Greece that God wants to use to take the gospel into all the world today.

"Greece was the first country to evangelize Russia, and now God has called her to help evangelize Russia once again. This is God's will for Greece. The money will be used for a noble purpose. You must let me take it out."

In the end, contrary to all regulations, I got to take the money out. It was a miracle.

From Athens, I flew to India, where another $200 was waiting for me. Earnestine was allowed to send only $200 per city, so she had sent me $200 in Athens and $200 in Visakhapatnam.

In addition to the second $200, I got another surprise in Visakhapatnam. The little Greek church had given me $1,000 because they had heard me testify about preaching the gospel to Russians, but I had not actually planned a trip to Russia during the remainder of my trip. Visakhapatnam, however, is right on the Bay of Bengal. Union Carbide does most of their shrimping off Visakhapatnam, and the Russian fleet was also there. When I checked into my hotel, I found that most of the other guests were Russians! I was over-joyed: God had arranged it so that I could reach two nations simultaneously. I had a field day, witnessing to the members of the Russian fleet, telling my testimony and handing out English gospels. I knew that I was sowing seed that would multiply back home in Russia as the members of the fleet finished their tours of duty and returned to their homeland.

When I wasn't witnessing to the Russians, I was setting up my crusade. Few people realize all the hard work that goes into a crusade before it even starts. There are many mundane details like choosing a time that will not conflict with local events (or fall in the local rainy season), choosing the right place to hold the crusade, obtaining the necessary permissions, scheduling the advertising, getting the hand-bills and posters printed and the banners painted, arranging for the handbills to be passed out on schedule and in the right places, getting a platform built and the sound and lighting systems set up, arranging for the cooperation of the local churches in finding and training volunteers to handle the crowd, fasting and praying for the crusade's success, and a host of other details. I threw myself into the work, using the money the Greek church had given me, along with what had come in since then.

Finally, it was almost done. I was just about ready for the good part—the crusade itself—when the Lord spoke to me: "Give the crusade to Ray Jennings." Ray Jennings, the man who had accompanied me on my first trip to India, had been helping with the preparations.

"But Lord!"

"Give the crusade to Ray Jennings."

"But Lord! Look at all the work I've done! Look at all the money I've spent! And Ray Jennings doesn't even know how to preach to get souls saved."

"Then teach him how," the Lord commanded.

Ray Jennings was an excellent teacher, but his subject at that time was church order. If you preach church order, you get excellent church order, but you don't get very many souls saved! Ray's ministry was to the church, I thought. But evidently the Lord thought otherwise.

"Brothers," I told the local church authorities, "I am not going to preach the crusade after all. Ray Jennings will preach instead of me."

The other ministers liked the idea as little as I did.

"But Brother Panos," one protested, "we have seen Ray Jennings preach, and there are no miracles. He is a teacher, not a preacher."

"When the Lord and I get through with him, he will be a preacher," I responded.

I taught Ray all I knew how to teach him, and then I left Visakhapatnam for Bangkok. I didn't even wait for the crusade. Later, word reached me that Ray's crusade had been a great success. Many souls had been saved, and many people had been healed. God's word had triumphed once again.

Bangkok lies in a sweeping bend of the Chao Phraya River, a conglomeration of concrete and glass office buildings, gold-topped Buddhist temples, modern housing projects, and incredible slums. Because it is laced by a system of klongs, or canals, it has been called the Venice of the East. Today, the klongs are rapidly being paved over to help solve Bangkok's traffic and sewage problems, but there are still many portions of the city which are inaccessible except by water. I didn't need a boat, though, to reach my destination. Despite the fact that I'd used all the money I'd received in Greece, I planned to stay at the Rama Hilton, following God's leading.

"I would like a single," I said to the clerk, "priced as reasonably as possible."

"I'm sorry, Mr. Panos, but we have no rooms available at this time. However, we do have a letter waiting here for you."

I took the letter and turned to go, wondering why God had sent me to the Hilton. As I turned I saw a familiar face: it was a friend of mine named Keith, whom I had met in Hong Kong.

"Keith!" I said, "what are you doing here?"

"Working. What are *you* doing here?"

I told Keith about my trip.

"Where are you staying?" Keith asked.

"I don't know. They're full up here. I think I'll try the YMCA."

"Don't do that," said Keith. "Stay with me. I'm designing a new wing for the Rama Hilton, and they've given me a suite to live in while I work for them."

It had been another of God's coincidences, which are really not coincidences at all. "I'm having a basket of fruit sent up," Keith told me. "I remember how much you like fruit. There are fruits here in Bangkok that you'll never see anywhere else."

Sure enough, I'd never seen anything like the fruit in Bangkok: some of it didn't look edible, but tasted delicious; other kinds looked beautiful and didn't taste edible. In addition to the strange Thai fruits with their unpronounceable names, there were also mangoes and oranges and lichee nuts. Before I left, Keith gave me an offering of a thousand bok, roughly equivalent to fifty dollars. God had replenished my fifty-dollar bankroll.

From Bangkok, I flew on to Kai Tak airport on Hong Kong's Kowloon side. While I was in Hong Kong, I was asked to preach. The church where I spoke gave me an offering, and I also received a large offering from a Chinese lady named Mrs. Fung. Mrs. Fung also bought me ten new suits! I had been window shopping, wishing I had the money to buy some of Hong Kong's cheap but well-made custom-tailored suits. I hadn't really prayed about it, but then I didn't have to pray. The Bible tells us that if we delight ourselves in the Lord, He will give us the desires of our hearts. He provided that desire through Mrs. Fung. Through another Christian, he provided three new pairs of shoes to go with the suits.

With the money I received in offerings, I bought my airline tickets home. I also bought perfume for Earnestine and gifts for the children. When I was through, I still had fifty dollars left. I headed homeward with stopovers in Hawaii and Los Angeles, content at last with my fifty-dollar bankroll. If the Lord could get me around the world on only fifty dollars, I thought, I wouldn't need to worry about His providing once I was back home in Houston. It seemed to be the decision the Lord was waiting for. In Los Angeles, I received an offering when I preached at a famous cathedral there, and back in Houston, I found a number of offerings waiting for me. Knowing I was on my way back home, Earnestine had not attempted to forward them to me. God was indeed providing "according to His riches in glory."

Chapter Twenty-Five
Target: Europe

Except for one thing, Earnestine was the perfect wife. I had loved her from our first meeting. She had prayed me into the kingdom of heaven. She was sweet and gracious, a good Christian, an excellent wife and mother. As the years passed, she seemed to grow even more beautiful. But I was disappointed that God had not called Earnestine to evangelize the lost.

I wanted Earnestine by my side as I traveled, but Earnestine hated to rough it. The trip to Mexico had been the last straw for her.

"Chris," Earnestine said, "I know God has called you to do what you're doing. But He hasn't called me. I feel like He's given me the job of being a wife and mother. He's given me our children to take care of. We can't just pull them out of school or dump them with relatives every time you go abroad. You go on without me. I don't see what good I'd do there anyway."

And that's how we left it for a while. Earnestine fasted

and prayed for me whenever I went overseas. I was grateful for her support. But I didn't just want her prayers. I wanted my helpmate by my side.

Except for praying about it, I let the matter rest for several years. Almost overnight, it seemed, the children grew. When Georganna was sixteen and Chrissy was thirteen, I decided to try again.

"It's about time we all did something together as a family," I told Earnestine. "How would you like to go to Europe? We won't go behind the iron curtain, we can stay in civilized hotels, and we'll go in summer, so we can take the kids."

"Are you going to be preaching or vacationing?"

"Both. I have a few preaching engagements, and we can do some sightseeing in between."

Earnestine wasn't enthusiastic about the idea, but she agreed to go. But there was more to it than that. She hadn't mentioned anything to me about it, but for some time she had been having pains in her chest. They hadn't seemed bad enough for her to see a doctor, but they worried her nevertheless.

"What if you get ill overseas?" the devil would ask her. "What if you can't find an English-speaking doctor? What if you actually *die* over there? Why, they'll have to ship your body home. Just think how expensive that will be!"

Earnestine is the kind of woman who keeps everything inside. She didn't mention a word of this to me. I knew she didn't seem very happy about the trip, but I put it down to the hardships of our trip to Mexico.

"Don't worry, darling," I teased her. "Europe isn't Mexico. Why, I bet we probably won't find a single dirt-floor hotel on the whole trip!"

Just as I promised, the European trip was a whole lot easier than the Mexican trip, although it was far from being a vacation. We had to do some pretty fast traveling to keep up with my rugged preaching schedule, but we got a lot of sightseeing in as well.

In Frankfurt, we all stayed at the Lofferts'. The Lofferts met us at the bus station and brought us home with them.

That Sunday, I preached in Brother Lofferts' church. They had several meetings during the week that I was there, and Earnestine, Georganna, and Chrissy gave their testimonies. Little Chrissy stole the show. He did so well that everyone asked me whether I'd told him what to say ahead of time. I hadn't, but the Holy Spirit had.

We had been so busy in Frankfurt that we had not had time to do very much sightseeing, but we made up for that deficiency in Rotterdam. There we visited the art museum. We took a tour of the canals. We visited a factory in Delft to see how they make that blue Delft china and a shoe shop to see how wooden shoes are made.

We saw the Skinny Bridge and the Weeping Tower, both dating from the seventeenth century. The bridge was indeed skinny; but the Weeping Tower didn't weep. It got its name because it had been the place where families saw their soldiers off to war. There were few windmills left in Holland, but there were flowers everywhere, a riot of color against the lush green grass.

From Rotterdam, we took a train to Copenhagen. When we got to the North Sea, they just loaded the train right on a boat. The kids and I got out and looked around, enjoying the salt sea breeze as whitecaps foamed on the choppy, gray-green sea.

In Copenhagen, we met Brother Clausson. He was ninety years old, but he had twenty-twenty vision and perfect hearing. He has one of the kindest faces I've ever seen, and a sweet, sweet spirit.

"I have been waiting all my life for you to come," he told me when we were introduced. "I want what you have. I am a

Christian, but I do not have the power that you have. It just seems as though something is missing, something that you have."

"I have nothing special," I told him. "It's God's power, not my power, but I will be happy to pray for you. God is not a respecter of persons. He is not in the business of withholding blessings from His children."

I prayed with Brother Clausson and God touched him in a mighty way. He laughed and wept as God filled him with a sense of His presence.

On the day we left, Brother Clausson accompanied us to the station. "Are you tired?" I asked as we made the long trip.

"Who, me?" he asked, his blue eyes twinkling. "I am fine. Are *you* tired?" He took the steps at the station as though he were nine instead of ninety.

Before we boarded the train, he handed me an envelope. "Here, take this," he said. It was a note wishing us Godspeed and quoting the Berkeley translation of 3 John 6: "You will do well to send them forward on their journey in a way befitting God's service." In addition to the note, the envelope contained three hundred crowns, about sixty dollars.

"Please," I said, "I can't accept this."

"You must," he said.

"Are you sure you don't need it?"

"Jesus Christ is my supplier," he answered. "He will give me more. He is a faithful God."

He hugged us, gave us some cookies to eat on the train, and said goodbye. As the train moved away, Brother Clausson stood on the platform, waving his handkerchief. Georganna and I burst into tears as he receded out of sight. Brother Clausson had just overflowed with love. He was a highlight of the trip.

From Denmark, we traveled on to Brussels, where we

toured a lace factory, and Paris, where we saw the sights. When we weren't sightseeing, I was preaching.

The kids enjoyed every moment of the trip, but it soon became clear that Earnestine was just along for the ride. She wanted to be where we were, but she would have been far happier if we'd been at home in Houston instead of gallivanting all around Europe. And then in Italy, Earnestine got sick.

Actually, Earnestine had already had several attacks of chest pain. Mostly they would hit in the middle of the night. She would lie in bed, gasping for breath. According to her, I would often just reach over in my sleep, still snoring, and bind the devil without ever waking up. Whenever I did this, the pain would disappear until the next attack. I knew little about this, however, as she'd only had one attack while I was awake. For two hours, Earnestine walked the floor, moaning and crying with the pain as I prayed. Finally, the attack subsided and we went to bed. So far as I knew, that was the only attack she'd had. She hadn't told me about the others.

When I was in Rome, Chrissy and I went to have an audience with the pope. As soon as we'd left the hotel that morning, Earnestine began to have another attack. She woke Georganna.

"Georganna, I'm not feeling well at all," Earnestine said. "Let's go downstairs. Maybe if I get out and see people, I'll forget about myself."

Georganna got dressed and she and Earnestine headed downstairs. On the way down, they saw a nurse. Earnestine hadn't even thought about the possibility of there being a nurse in the hotel.

"Is there a doctor in this hotel?" Earnestine asked.

"Yes, there is," the nurse replied. "Are you having problems?"

"Well," said Earnestine, "I feel like I just can't catch my

215

breath. And I can't feel my pulse. And I have this pain in my chest and arm."

"Well, come on down," the nurse said, "and let me check you."

In her office, the nurse held Earnestine's wrist. "Do you feel any pulse?" Earnestine asked her.

"Oh, yes," the nurse said, "but it is very slow. And due to the pain in your right arm, I think I should call the doctor."

Earnestine returned to her room to await the doctor. He must have arrived only shortly before my return, because when I came back from my audience with the pope, it looked like Earnestine was on her death bed. She was lying on the divan in our hotel room, and the doctor was hovering over her.

"Don't worry," God said, "there's nothing wrong with her. She's just bound by a spirit of fear."

I walked up to the doctor and said, "Doctor, there's nothing wrong with her. It's a spirit of fear, and I command that thing to leave her body in the name of Jesus."

The doctor took it all in his stride and went on checking her. In a few minutes he said, "Mrs. Panos, I can find nothing at all the matter with you. All you need is a little fresh air."

When the doctor left, Earnestine was indignant.

"Chris Panos," she stormed, "you are the limit! Here I am dying, with a doctor hovering over me, and you don't even care. You just barge right in and tell the doctor there's nothing wrong with me. He must think I'm some kind of hypochondriac!"

She was embarrassed, but I didn't care what the doctor thought. I was happy she was alive and well and out of pain. Fortunately for me, she didn't stay miffed for very long, and soon we were on our way again. We went back for another week at the Lofferts' church in Frankfurt, then headed home.

"Traveling just isn't for me, Chris," she told me as we jetted back across the Atlantic. "If I can just get back home once more, I never want to leave the United States again."

I was crestfallen. I had hoped that the trip to Europe would whet Earnestine's appetite for the foreign field. Instead, it had worked in reverse. To her, Europe was just like America, with a little additional inconvenience thrown in. She still saw no point in accompanying me as I evangelized.

"Lord," I prayed, "you've got to do something. She's my wife. You gave her to me. I know you want her with me as a helpmate."

I knew He would in His own good time. Meanwhile, I continued to storm the gates of heaven in prayer.

Chapter Twenty-Six
Another Spy for God

Within months of our trip to Europe, God dealt with Earnestine on the subject of travel. She was miserable. She didn't want to leave the States, but she didn't want to disobey God either. Soon, she told the Lord that she would go wherever He sent her.

Not long after her new commitment, she accompanied me to a meeting where I was speaking.

"I'm getting ready for another series of crusades in India," I told the people, "and I just feel like my wife should go along. What do you think?"

"Oh, Lord, I hope this isn't the time," Earnestine prayed. "But I'll stick to my promise. I will do whatever you want. If they give us the money for me to go too, I know I'll have to go. But oh, Lord, I hope they don't give us the money for me!"

They gave us the money.

Earnestine sent Georganna and Chrissy to stay with her

219

parents, and we took off for points East. The flight went well
at first. Then the pilot came on the intercom. "We are passing over Paris," he announced.

"Oh, Lord, what have I done?" Earnestine asked herself.
"Not nine months ago, I said if I could just get back home I
would never leave the States again. And here I am flying
over Paris! What have I done?"

From then on, the flight was pretty rough for Earnestine.
She began to think about India. Earnestine is very tender-
hearted. She had heard me tell about the terrible conditions,
and she dreaded having to see all the sickness, poverty, and
sorrow. She was sick at heart.

We landed briefly in Bombay, where we caught another
plane to Hyderabad.

"Chris, did you see those airport guards?" I had seen the
guards but I hadn't thought too much about them.

"What about them?"

"Oh, Chris, they were so pitiful, with their bare feet and
their wrinkled uniforms, and their big brown eyes."

The guards' uniforms were wrinkled because they were in
the habit of napping between airplanes.

"Oh, Lord," I prayed, "if she thinks the guards are pitiful,
wait till she sees the cripples and the beggars!"

In Hyderabad, a party of Indians met us at the airport.
We chatted, than took a taxi to our hotel.

"See?" I asked Earnestine. "Nothing to it! Why, we're not
even smuggling anything. If you think this is bad, you should
try carrying a few hundred gospels across the Russian border sometime."

Earnestine shuddered. "Oh , Chris," she moaned, "you're
not thinking of taking me behind the iron curtain, are you?"

I laughed. "Not yet, anyway. I was just trying to get you
to count your blessings. You look so glum."

"I dreaded coming to India because I had heard of all the

suffering and sorrow here. And now that I actually see it, it's worse then anything I'd ever dreamed!"

It was about six o'clock in the morning, and our taxi ride took us past row upon row of homeless street dwellers—young and old, men and women—all sleeping out in the open on the sidewalk, many with no covering other than the clothes on their backs. Here and there, some were starting to awake. Earnestine watched one man as he moved painfully along. He had no legs. He walked on his hands, his body dragging along the ground.

"I had no idea," Earnestine said. "To think of these people living in such miserable, pitiful conditions all their lives, only to go to hell when they die. I can't bear to think about it. Somehow, they must hear the gospel!"

One look at India had done more for Earnestine than all my preaching. The more she saw, the more burdened she became.

The following day, we proceeded on our journey. We traveled through the blasting heat of the desert along a single-lane "highway." Once, a huge truck ran our car off the road and into a muddy bank of sand, but God was with us. There was no damage.

Earnestine drank in the sights. She saw women construction workers building a single-lane highway in that devastating heat, carrying gravel in baskets on their heads. She saw lepers with their toes and fingers worn to stumps, women beggars with deformed babies on their hips, child beggars of only five or six, seemingly parentless. A hundred times a day, it seemed as though Earnestine's heart would break. It seemed like mine would, too. At night we wept into our pillows, crying out to God.

Night after night, we continued to pray. The answer, when it came a week later, was totally unexpected.

"You've been here a week," the Lord said. "What makes

My evangelists think they can flit into a country for a week or ten days and then say they've reached that country for the gospel?"

"What do you want me to do, Lord?"

"I want you to make disciples," He said. "I want you to teach the nationals how to preach the gospel. I want you to mass the nationals and preach to them, not just one time but many times. I want you to keep coming back to India again and again and again, until the national evangelists catch on how to preach the gospel."

The nationals! It was the answer Earnestine and I were praying for.

"Oh, Chris, that's it!" Earnestine cried when I told her what the Lord had said. "You can raise up nationals, and they can raise up nationals, and the ones that they raise up can raise up others. I just knew the Lord would show us a way! Oh, I am so thankful!"

I was thankful too.

It's a good thing God gave Earnestine a burden for souls, because the first night of the first crusade she saw me preach in India, I was a total flop. It was a fiasco.

Even in the big Indian cities like Delhi, there are no arenas as we know them. Mass political rallies and sports events are held on large open plots of ground called *maidan*. Except on the platforms, there are no seats on these maidan. People either stand or squat on the ground to hear the speakers. Any dignitaries who attend are given seats on the speakers' platform.

In Caddapa, our platform was huge. Everything started out well. I was happy. God had answered my prayers, and I had my wife beside me. There were about ten thousand people in the crowd.

As soon as I mounted the platform, my good mood disappeared. The platform wasn't built right. Instead of using plywood on top, they had used bamboo. That wasn't all. The whole thing swayed from side to side as I walked on it.

The platform obviously wouldn't hold as many as I'd intended, so I instructed the workers to seat the dignitaries and choir on the ground. After some hustle and bustle, we got everything reorganized. I started to preach. Then it happened. The platform began to sway. I took a step to steady myself and my leg sank through the bamboo.

"Oh, no," I thought. "Now what!" One of the Indians pulled me out of the hole. Gingerly, I moved to the front of the platform and started to speak. Then all the lights went out. Workers hurried to connect the sound system to the car batteries we had on hand for emergencies. By the time the lights and the sound were working again, the platform had collapsed. We canceled the service.

Earnestine was sympathetic, but I was mortified. As soon as we got back to the government house, I went to prayer. "Oh, Lord, look what happened! Why did you let it happen?"

"Why did *you* let it happen?" the Lord replied. Lovingly, He showed me that I was never to take anything for granted during a crusade. If I had checked the construction of that platform as it was being built, I wouldn't have been embarrassed by having it collapse.

I spent the next day putting things back together. A team of carpenters had worked all night resurfacing the platform and reinforcing its underpinnings. It didn't look terribly elegant, but I was sure it was sturdy enough to hold not only me, but the invited dignitaries also.

Amazingly, even though I hadn't preached the night before, the crowds had doubled. Rain clouds massed, but I took authority over the gathering storm. It looked, then, as though a giant lasso had roped off the crusade grounds, or as though angels had formed a ring around it. There were clouds and rain all over the surrounding areas, but not one drop touched us. Overhead the sky was bright and clear.

After the message, I prayed for the sick. One little crippled boy came to the platform to testify. One of his feet was turned under, but God had healed his arm, which had been deformed. As he testified, his foot straightened out before our eyes. It was the first miracle like that that Earnestine had ever seen. She actually watched as the foot straightened right before her eyes. All that remained of his affliction were a few leathery callouses on the top of his foot where it had dragged along the ground.

"Chris," she told me later, "I felt like I was back in Bible times. God's power became so real to me."

So many cripples were healed that second night that it reminded me of a stampede. As they hurried forward, dust filled the air. They leaped and ran and jumped for joy. Thousands raised their hands to accept Jesus as Lord.

Sunday night as I began to preach, seven demon-possessed women broke through the ropes around the platform area. They rushed straight at me, shouting and cursing. I sneaked a look at Earnestine. Her eyes opened wide as she looked at the women. Then suddenly she closed her eyes and bowed in prayer.

"Fall down in the name of Jesus," I commanded the women. They fell where they were. One dropped just as she was entering the enclosure in front of the platform. She collapsed onto the ropes, where she hung limply till the end of the service.

After I finished preaching, I led the crowd in the sinners' prayer. Then I turned to the seven women. "In the name of Jesus Christ, the Son of God, I command you to rise."

They rose. They stood there quietly, restored to normal. I led them in the sinners' prayer. They prayed and accepted Jesus into their hearts. Many had been insane for years.

Some had actually had to be chained to trees because of their insanity. Now they were well. One by one, they began to weep and praise the Lord. We brought them to the microphone, and let them testify to the crowd.

"This is not my work," I said to the crowd. "I am not doing these miracles myself. I have no power apart from God. What you see is God's power. It is happening because God is God."

The next night, I invited a national preacher to preach. I make a practice of doing this, not only to give the nationals valuable experience, but also to prove to the worshipers that I have no special power, that the power lies in God.

The night the national spoke, the miracles continued. The next night, another national preached and there were even more miracles. God was confirming His word.

The nightly meetings, and the nightly miracles, were still going on long after we returned to Houston. God had answered my prayers "above all that I was able to ask or think."

Earnestine had received a soul-winner's heart. We had spied out the land of India, and, like God's spies in the Book of Numbers we could come back to God's people and say, "Let us go up at once and possess the land, for we are well able to overcome it."

Earnestine had become another spy for God.

Chapter Twenty-Seven
The Blue-Eyed Affair

I spent some time at home, enjoying my family and speaking at various places in the States, but as winter turned into spring I began to feel the call of Communist countries once again. Soon I was on my way to Moscow.

The flight was easy, and clearing customs was almost routine. Once again, I prayed, "blinding" the customs agents' eyes. Once again, they saw nothing as they inspected my bags. After clearing customs, I traveled on into the center of Moscow and checked into the Metropole Hotel again. That Sunday, I returned to the Baptist church.

"When you arrive at the church," the Lord told me, "two of the deacons are going to recognize you from your last visit. They are going to ask you to sit with them up in the balcony. Do not go with them. Bind them and blind them in the name of Jesus, as you did the customs agents. Then circulate among the congregation downstairs. As you do, I will show you the people to whom you must give the New Testaments you have brought."

Everything happened just as the Lord had said. When I got to the church, two of the deacons converged on me. "Come on up and sit with us," they said.

"I bind you and blind you in Jesus' name," I responded. Without waiting to see what they would do, I turned my back on them and walked quickly into the crowd of worshipers on the main floor of the church. Moving slowly because of the crush, I made my way through the mass of people handing gospels and New Testaments to those God pointed out.

"Walk over there," the Lord said.

I went in the direction He had indicated and as I did I saw a little blonde woman. She had a notebook, and she was writing just as fast as she could write.

Because most of them are unable to own Bibles, Russian believers have an enormous hunger for the word of God. When they attend church, they copy down whatever Scriptures the pastor happens to mention in his sermon. That is what this woman was doing; she was painfully gleaning a precious store of Scripture seed from the nearly barren field of the pastor's sermon.

When I got to the lady, I handed her one of my New Testaments. She looked up at me with the brightest, bluest eyes that I have ever seen. As I watched, those beautiful blue eyes just flooded with tears. She started to weep and praise God with a thankfulness most of us have probably never experienced. And then a miracle took place: it was as though, when I looked in that woman's eyes, I saw in some way the eyes of Jesus Himself. I have never seen such love, such joy, such beauty, in any person's eyes before or since. And they responded over just one little New Testament.

Soon, God drew me away from that beautiful blue-eyed saint. Following His guidance, I went back against the wall of the sanctuary, near one of the posts holding up the balcony.

When the service ended I just leaned back against the wall and handed out New Testaments as the crowd went by. Soon, one of the ministers saw what I was doing. "Stop! Stop! Stop!" he shouted, walking in my direction. He looked angry enough to strangle me.

"I bind you and blind you in Jesus' name," I said. And a miracle took place. Instantly, the man began to smile.

"Where have you been?" he asked. "I haven't seen you in a while." He remembered me from my last visit. My offense forgotten, we chatted for a while.

That minister wasn't the only one who noticed what I was doing. I was followed when I left the church. Two blocks later, the man caught up with me and grabbed my sleeve.

"I saw what you were doing," he said. I felt a sudden stab of alarm.

"Please, do you have one left that you can give to me?"

Thankful that I had one left to give to him, I handed the man a New Testament. He had risked much—imprisonment or maybe life itself—to get it.

While I was staying at the Metropole, I met a dentist and his wife from Atlanta, Georgia. Dr. and Mrs. Thompson were born-again believers. We chatted a bit and got to know one another. The following Sunday, I met Dr. Thompson at the Baptist church. This time, I had allowed the elders to conduct me to the elders' room before the service. There, I ran into Dr. Thompson. They had spotted him for a foreigner, and were trying to con him out of any Bibles he might have with him.

"Don't give them any Bibles," I said to him. "They're just compromisers. If you give them Bibles, they'll just lock them up in the safe right there, and that will be the last any Christian ever sees of them."

Later, back at the Metropole, I described my Bible-smuggling activities to the dentist and his wife. I told them about the time I'd seen the safe in the elders' office chock full of confiscated Bibles. He was fascinated; she looked nervous. Soon I had a chance to give them a live demonstration.

We had all gone to the world-famous Bolshoi Ballet, which is possibly the best in the world. It was a flawless performance. The dancers were exquisite that night, and the orchestra was superb.

I had worn my overcoat to the performance, partly because I needed something to ward off the cool night air, and partly because it was stuffed with New Testaments. I didn't want to miss even a single chance that might arise to hand them out.

When intermission came, I prayed for guidance as we walked to the lobby.

"Talk to the Russian officers," the Lord said. "They are almost never witnessed to. Tell them about Jesus."

There was a Russian officer standing a few feet from me, looking very sure of himself in his crisp, perfectly-tailored uniform. His chest was full of medals, his posture was erect and his boots shone to perfection.

"I want to tell you about Jesus," I said. I slipped a New Testament into his hand as I shook it. Like most Russian officers, he understood English well. He listened intently as I explained that God had told me to witness to him. We didn't talk long; there were too many other Russian officers there that night. I spent the whole intermission going from one to another handing out New Testaments, accompanied by a few short words of testimony. Nobody raised an outcry. All the officers listened politely, and each accepted the little New Testament I pressed into his hand. I knew I was being protected by the power of God.

Dr. and Mrs. Thompson watched as I circulated among the Russian officers. She kept tugging on his sleeve, trying to get him to leave. During the remainder of our stay in the Metropole, they kept a respectful distance away from me, but later, back in the States, Dr. Thompson invited me to speak to a meeting of Christian businessmen in Atlanta. Safe at home, Mrs. Thompson was able to laugh about her fears.

I saw Dr. and Mrs. Thompson again that trip, but not in Russia. The Czechoslovakians were staging an uprising, and Russian troops were massed at the Czechoslovakian borders, ready to quell the revolt.

When I heard the news, I felt impressed to go and be with the Czechoslovakians in their time of need. I made a brief stopover in Vienna to obtain Czechoslovakian and Russian gospels of John, and then boarded a plane for Prague.

"I want you to take those gospels through," the Lord told me aboard the plane, "and when you walk through the customs, I want you to blind them as you did the Russian customs agents. But this time you're not going to have any difficulty."

When the plane landed, I went towards the customs area with my blue suitcase in one hand and my brown bag in the other hand. As I walked, I prayed silently, blinding the customs agent and binding the powers of darkness. As soon as I got near the customs agent, I waved at him, meanwhile switching my bags from hand to hand. Suddenly, I felt as though I were being filled with a divine anointing of love for that particular customs agent. I beamed at him as I passed him. He smiled back. I must have been walking, but I felt as though I was just floating along, almost as though I were on one of those moving sidewalks that they have in certain airports. As I floated on into Prague, I saw Dr. and Mrs. Thompson, going in the opposite direction. I was entering Prague, and they were leaving. We were in two different streams of traffic so it was impossible for us to stop and talk.

I had gotten through customs and was going to change my

money at the bank when I realized that I had gone through customs without getting my bags inspected, and without even getting my passport stamped. I couldn't believe that it had been so simple.

I don't know what made me do it, but I turned around, went back to the customs area, and got in line again. It was almost like a rerun. I walked back on through the customs area again, shifted my bags again, and waved at that same guard again. Again, I felt like I was on a conveyor belt, and again the guard smiled at me and waved me through without stamping my passport.

When I came out of the customs area for the second time, there was Pavlicek. He was just standing there, scanning the incoming crowds as though he was waiting for someone. When he saw me, he was overjoyed.

"You are like an angel sent from God," he said.

I never did ask him what or whom he'd been waiting for, but I think that the Holy Spirit sent him there to wait for me. He accompanied me to the bank to get my money changed, and then we left the airport.

God moved in a mighty way that trip. I spoke in a forest outside of Prague. When Pavlicek and I arrived, the forest seemed to be deserted. Suddenly, the people started to arrive. It looked as though they came out of nowhere. No meeting had been announced, but thousands came, led by the Holy Spirit.

I spoke words of encouragement, telling the Czechoslovakians to be strong, and reminding them that the Russian soldiers needed to be witnessed to. After that, many Czechoslovakians were encouraged to witness to the Russian soldiers. I, too, was able to speak to many and gave them the Russian gospels.

"It means so much to us, just to have known that someone cares," the Christians told me over and over again. "We have felt so alone in our struggle. We felt as though nobody knew, nobody cared. We are so happy that you came."

One day during that trip, I happened to be speaking in a cherry orchard. Once again, it was an unannounced, open-air meeting. The day was very warm. After I spoke, some of the men climbed the cherry trees and gave me fresh, tree-ripened cherries, still warm from the late summer sun.

Being given cherries by a group of iron curtain Christians reminded me of another incident that had happened not too long before. I had been in Hungary. There, I had spoken during strawberry season. The couple with whom I had stayed had owned a strawberry farm.

Usually, I try not to stay with iron curtain Christians. It is too dangerous for them. The KGB interrogates any iron-curtain national who entertains a foreigner of any sort, both to see if his ideology has been contaminated by contact with the West, and also to see if the national can be recruited to spy for the KGB against the foreigner should the foreigner have any further contact with him.

When I was invited to stay with the couple who owned the strawberry farm, I had remonstrated with them.

"It is much too dangerous for you," I said. "You are running a big risk."

"Yes," Mr. Imre said, "we know. But there is no hotel in our small town, and the people are hungry for the gospel. We do not care about the risks; please come."

And so I had gone to stay with the Imre family, praying that God would give them protection. Night after night, I preached in the Imres' little cottage. I am used to pacing as I preach, often gesticulating to emphasize my point. At the Imres', I couldn't pace; I could hardly stand. The cottage was so crowded that I had to hold my feet together as I preached. We were packed like sardines in the little house.

In spite of the risks, the Imres were overjoyed to have me.

They gave me fresh-picked strawberries morning, noon, and night. I had strawberry cakes, strawberry juice, and fresh strawberries with cream. They were delicious. When I finished preaching, the grandmother accompanied me to the train station, taking a terrible risk just to see me off.

"You mustn't do this," I said.

"Oh, yes, I must," she answered. "You have come all the way from America to preach the gospel to us. I cannot let you find your way to the station alone."

All too soon we heard my train approaching.

"Come back soon," Grandmother Imre told me. "This is what Hungary needs—what all the world needs. We need the gospel of Jesus Christ. Do not forget us when you go back to America."

Chapter Twenty-Eight
An Angel in Disguise

Back at home, I began to pray and plan for my next move. As I made more and more crusades overseas and my need for funds increased, my list of supporters increased as well. I had set up a non-profit corporation called Release the World for Christ so that those who donated to the work could receive an income tax deduction. In addition. I wanted them to know how their money was being spent. Soon there were too many to keep in touch with personally. To cope with the situation, I began sending out a little newsletter called the *Far East Reporter*. Response was so enthusiastic that it wasn't long before the *Far East Reporter* became a twelve-page tabloid newspaper accredited by the Evangelical Press Association.

When I say response was enthusiastic, I suppose I should qualify that. Response from our *supporters* was enthusiastic. Earnestine and I felt differently. We had no spare room in our little house, and after the *Reporter* started up, we felt as though we had no room of any kind! We had converted our attached garage into an office where the *Far East Reporter* and other materials were written and readied for print, but even so, we were almost crowded out. Every available nook and cranny was put to use; it seemed as though you couldn't turn around without finding stacks of *Reporters* or bundles of correspondence or miscellaneous art supplies. I felt cramped for space, and I knew Earnestine did too. Earnestine is an excellent housekeeper, but it's hard to make any house look neat when it has stacks of newspapers in every corner. I began to pray about renting an office.

One day, as I was driving through downtown Houston, the Lord pointed out a building. "That's where your office is going to be," He said. It was a beautiful new office building in Houston's Cullen Center. I knew the rent would be astronomical. I went home and prayed about it. The more I prayed, the more I felt impressed that the Lord wanted us to rent the space.

"Earnestine," I said one morning, "I am going downtown to rent that office."

"Chris, where are you going to get the money? It will be an extra expense each month, and just think of the souls we could save with all those dollars!"

"We aren't going to win very many souls if we're buried under a sea of newspapers," I said. "And besides, if I rent an office, the Lord will be able to send us some helpers. If someone were to volunteer right now there wouldn't be any place that we could put them."

I went downtown to the Cullen Center. At the rental office, I explained that we were a non-profit Christian organization on very tight budget.

"I'll tell you what," the manager said. "I have an office that is standing empty right now. I can let you have it at half price, if you'll take it on a month-to-month basis. But if a firm comes along that wants it at the regular rate, I will have to give it to them."

"It's a deal!" I said joyfully. I knew that no other firm was going to come along as long as God wanted us in that particular office space. When we outgrew it, maybe the office would get a taker, but not before.

Within a week, God had provided office furniture. Some things were given to us, and others we bought at spectacular savings that "just happened" to be available, with money that "just happened" to arrive at that particular time.

Earnestine and I now had a great, big, beautiful office all to ourselves. We had no help, but in spite of our temporary labor shortage, we organized as though we had many employees. Earnestine took charge of the mail, opening it, recording contributions, sending out the receipts. As before, I edited the newspaper and managed the finances. Many bills were due, and the money wasn't coming in as it had been. I spent much time in prayer and asked the Lord for money to meet our needs.

One morning Earnestine and I were praying and praising God in our living room. Our faith was especially strong that morning, and we left for the office expecting some large donations to come in that day. But when Earnestine went down to get the mail, it consisted only of a single letter.

As she handed me the envelope, I noticed a note attached to the check. It asked if we needed any help in the office.

"Praise the Lord!" I thought. "We didn't get much money, but maybe we got a secretary to help out."

I called the phone number given in the letter, only to learn that the volunteer couldn't type. For some reason, I said, "Come on down Thursday morning at ten anyway. We'll find some way to put you to work."

That Thursday Earnestine had some errands to run and I

too was running late, but shortly after ten I found the volunteer patiently waiting in front of my locked office door. As soon as we were seated inside, I was bombarded by a series of questions about Release the World for Christ, especially about trust departments.

For the next half hour, I listened to a barrage of reasons why we needed a trust department. Finally Earnestine arrived at the office and rescued me from the volunteer.

"I have a stack of letters that need to be stuffed," Earnestine said. "If you're finished talking with Chris, perhaps you could help me with them."

Like most women, Earnestine enjoys talking about her family. "We have a daughter who will graduate from high school this year," Earnestine told the volunteer over the pile of letters. "But we have no funds to send her to college. My husband was very successful in business, but he sold everything to go and preach the gospel. I asked him to please set aside some money for the children's education, but he said no, God would provide for all our needs."

It is extremely unusual for Earnestine to bare her soul like that—especially to a stranger—but the Lord had a purpose in it. The following Thursday, the volunteer was back again, still talking about a trust department. Then the volunteer gave Earnestine the name and telephone number of the vice-president of a Christian university.

"A niece of mine knows him personally," the volunteer said, "and might be able to arrange a scholarship for your daughter."

Earnestine made the contact and Georganna got the scholarship. Gratefully, I began to pray, asking God for His leading concerning a trust department. Soon it was Thursday again.

"Where would we get the money to start this trust?" I asked the volunteer.

"I have some acreage that has some timber on it," the volunteer said. "The timber has been cut within the past ten years, so we can't expect too much, but God can even grow timber. Let's pray and ask God to prosper the land and what we get from the sale of the timber will be the beginning of our trust fund."

So we set our hearts on God, praying without ceasing. In the meantime, the volunteer contacted four lumber companies for bids. A bid for $18,000 came in immediately from Georgia Pacific. Several months later, they raised their bid to $25,000. We continued to pray. One morning I saw a truck that had "Georgia Pacific" on the side of it as I was driving to the office.

"That is the company that will buy the timber," the Lord said. Upon arriving at the office, I phoned the volunteer.

"You will sell your timber to Georgia Pacific," I said. "Ask them for another bid."

"All right," the volunteer replied, "but I am going to sell it to the highest bidder, Georgia Pacific or no Georgia Pacific."

"That's fine with me," I said.

The volunteer contacted all four lumber companies and set a date for final bids to be submitted. Sure enough, Georgia Pacific raised theirs to $30,000, the highest of the four. Release the World for Christ now had a trust department.

In the early days of my ministry I had spent many hours writing. Soon I accumulated a number of different manuscripts. One Thursday, I asked the volunteer to take the script of *Faith Under Fire* home to read. "You must send this to a publisher," the volunteer reported back. "It is one of the best books I've ever read."

Faith Under Fire was published and became a best seller in forty-five days. Soon, other books were published: *How You Can Have a Miracle Ministry, How to be Led by the Spirit, How to Pray,* and *How to Have Power.*

Months sped by as I divided my time between home and overseas. One Thursday morning the volunteer told me, "You are going to get a new office. I had a vision that this office became so small that we opened the window and stepped out on a board over the street."

A few days later the lease manager notified me that someone wanted our office. We went to prayer. Soon the lease manager told us of a Christian bonding company which had three years left on a lease in Cullen Center and wanted to move. The company let us have their lease at half price, and they also sold us much of the furniture in the office at great savings.

Soon the Lord began to prosper us, and we were able to purchase a small printing press and a machine for duplicating tapes. I had been recording my messages at various speaking engagements; now I was able to offer them to people who had not been able to attend.

Through tapes, I could minister in homes across America even at times when I myself was overseas. It was a foretaste of what the Lord was about to do for our ministry through the use of modern technology.

The best was yet to come.

Chapter Twenty-Nine
Tell the Lady That I Love Her

We were up to our ears in work, planning a Miracle Life Conference to be held in Houston, when the volunteer sprang another bit of news.

"You are going on television. I saw you behind a pulpit in the air with scenes from around the world."

For years I had wanted to go on television. I believe now that it was the Lord who had put the desire in my heart. But when the volunteer spoke to me about it, I nearly dismissed the idea. "Why, He could get trained men who have experience on TV already. What would He want with me?"

But the thought stuck in my mind. After the conference, the Lord began to speak to me some more. "You've heard it said that every generation belongs to its talkers," He reminded me. "This has been true throughout the history of mankind. Leadership implies speakership. People have always come together to share news, to get information, to talk about their problems and ideas.

"Today, it's the media which are the common gathering

places for this generation. Instead of influencing a handful in the barbershop or a few hundred in the town hall or in a church, television speaks to millions.

"The pulpit and the pew are important to Christians, but they are not the major gathering place for the rank and file. Television is. That is why it is so important. Through television, you will be able to influence not thousands, but millions."

Following the Lord's leading, I announced a meeting to raise funds for television. I had hoped for a big turnout, but when the time came, only eight showed up.

"You'll never get off the ground with just eight people," the devil snickered. "Television takes a lot of capital. Why, you'd be lucky to get enough for a thirty-second commercial out of a group this size, and here you've been planning to do half-hour shows."

It was a last-minute attempt to steal my faith, but it didn't work. I continued to believe God for the necessary finances as I shared my vision with the eight people who'd arrived. By the end of the meeting, $95,000 had been pledged.

We named the TV program "The Chris Panos Show." Christians, we reasoned, would soon come to hear about the show through word of mouth. It was the non-Christians we needed to attract, and a non-Christian would be turned off by a name that had a religious-sounding ring to it. So "The Chris Panos Show" it was.

"God has burdened Chris Panos to reach one billion souls behind the iron and bamboo curtains," says the TV announcer. "Fresh from recent journeys to these countries, where he has distributed Bibles and preached the living word, here is Chris Panos."

And there I am. I have come to think of "The Chris Panos Show" more as a church than a TV program. I don't want to give you the wrong idea; it definitely isn't a televised church service. It has a talk show format, and usually there's a song and a mini-sermon in addition to whatever else is happening. Often, Earnestine and I will interview the celebrities of the Christian world, men like David du Plessis and Harald Bredesen. Other times, we may show documentaries of overseas crusades. But always, no matter how else the show may vary, there are two constants: one is Jesus Christ, and the other is His word.

Each day, throughout the show, a telephone number flashes on the screen. This number is connected to a bank of telephones which are answered by dedicated Christian volunteers. People call in with every problem you can imagine. We get calls from heroin addicts, jobless fathers, would-be suicides, terminal cancer patients. Callers include Christians, backsliders, unbelievers, and people who want to come to know the Lord.

Often, as I preach across the air waves, I can sense waves of Holy Spirit power welling up inside of me and actually flooding out over the air waves to meet the needs of our television audience. Letters and phone calls tell of the results. We estimate that thirty-nine thousand souls were saved by the television show alone last year.

Sometimes, if there is an urgent need or an unusual testimony, the telephone counselors may refer callers to me right on the air. Most often, however, the counselors pray with the callers themselves, and remind the viewers that it is God and not Chris Panos whose power will meet their needs.

Some of the counselors have an almost full-time ministry stemming from the half-hour daily show. Two of the women have lists of people that they call after the show is over, to read the word of God to them. Some of our viewers cannot read. Others have questions about the Bible. Again, the

243

counselors handle most of these themselves. But after every show, and we're on live five days a week, there are always a few calls that the counselors feel I should handle personally. As I call these members of my TV audience, I feel like the pastor of a far-flung TV congregation.

Our initial investment disappeared quickly. After that, we depended on gifts from viewers and others to raise the necessary working capital. It was a constant battle to pray the money in, but when we saw the results, we realized that it was worth every penny that we spent on it.

Daily we take time out to pray for prayer requests that are phoned in. People tell me that they can feel the love that flows from the television screen as Earnestine and I lay hands on the requests and pray. One of the most satisfying parts of my ministry is hearing the reports of what God is doing for our TV audience. Arthritis, tumors, and fevers disappear. A three-year-old is cured of meningitis as her mother prays. A young boy misses the school bus, watches the show, and is healed of painfully blocked tear ducts. Families are reunited. Jobless fathers find work after prayer.

As the Bible puts it, "with God, nothing shall be impossible."

Chapter Thirty
Telegandi Bloodbath

Leaving Earnestine home with the children, I was off to India once more and headed for Nizamabad.

Nizamabad, India, is named after King Nizam, a Muslim ruler who was perhaps the richest man in the world in his day. His collection of jewels was world-famous. But Nizamabad was no jewel box when I went there. Instead, it was the site of a civil war between the Telegandi and the Andara Pradesh people. The Telegandi are a little darker than the Andara Pradesh, and they are considered to be of a lower caste. They claimed that they were being discriminated against in many ways, especially in the matter of employment.

The Telegandi uprising was a real bloodbath. Indira Gandhi had declared martial law, and the whole city had been closed down: the shops were closed, the schools were closed, even the movie houses were closed. Nizamabad was a political tinderbox.

I knew the danger, but I decided to go nevertheless. With

the whole town closed down, I reasoned, I would have a captive audience. People would come because there was nothing else for them to do.

Just as I expected, the whole town turned out to hear the gospel. Even the Hindus came. Many of the Hindus had brought their lizards with them. This is an old satanic trick. It is said that if the lizard sings, the speaker is telling the truth. The lizards "sang" like squeeking gates all through my sermon. Even the devil occasionally has to tell the truth.

Just as I began to preach, a one-eyed Arya Samaj came to the meeting with a rowdy group of Hindus. The Arya Samaj are a politically active radical Hindu sect.

"If your God is real, then heal my eye," he shouted. It was not his eye that he was concerned about, I knew; what he really wanted was an excuse to kill me or drive me out of the country. When his eye socket remained empty, the group rushed toward the platform, yelling "Kill him! Kill him!"

Just as they had almost reached the platform, I looked up and saw Jesus. He seemed to be about a hundred feet tall, and as I watched I saw Him lift one enormous hand, ready to act. Then He paused.

"Son," He said, "I'm going to teach you the most important lesson you've learned so far. I want you to change the atmosphere. Take authority over the principalities and powers and rulers of darkness. By your speech and preaching, you must demonstrate the power of God."

Then I saw it. I saw that the words the Arya Samaj had shouted—"Kill him! Kill him!"—had germinated in the air like seed. These satanically-inspired utterances had begun to dominate the whole crusade. Now it was up to me. I could either accept defeat, or fight their negative words with the positive words of God.

All this happened in what must have been just an instant of time. As I beheld Jesus, I bound the principalities and powers and rulers of spiritual darkness. The men who had been rushing at me halted in their tracks. Next I began to preach the Blood and the Cross. When I had finished my sermon, I led the people in the sinners' prayer and went on to pray for the sick. As I did, the one-eyed man started towards me once again.

"Stop, in the name of Jesus!" I commanded. He stopped right where he was.

On my right, a crippled man climbed on the platform as I watched. I had told my workers not to allow anybody on the platform, so his being there was most unusual. When I saw the man's faith, however, I commanded him to rise and walk. He not only rose, he leaped and ran up and down the platform. The crowd went wild.

Next a Telegandi woman stood up. "I am a Telegandi! I am a Telegandi!" she shouted. "God healed my baby! All you Telegandis, you must listen to this man!" She told us that the baby she was holding had suffered from an enormous goiter. When I prayed for the sick, the baby's goiter had disappeared before her eyes.

Soon, an Andara Pradesh had also received a miracle. He exhorted his people, too, to hear the word of God.

As the miracles continued, the crowd began to rally to my defense. There seemed to be some danger of a battle breaking out: not between the Telegandi and the Andara Pradesh this time, but between the Arya Samaj and the rest of the audience. I commanded the one-eyed ringleader of the Arya Samaj to leave the meeting. As he obeyed, he screamed out with a voice that sounded like a hundred devils yelling at one time. His voice was so loud it sounded like he had a public address system at his disposal as he shrieked in fear. Next, I walked to the edge of the platform and stretched my hands out towards his followers. They began to fall under the power of God. The frightened Christians begged me to leave. "We'll bring reproach on the name of Jesus with all this fuss," they said.

"Only when we are willing to be beaten and even to die for the sake of the gospel will we see victories," I told them. "Now is not the time to be lukewarm. Now is the time to stand your ground."

They stood. We finished the meeting in the usual manner. At the end, each member of the tour got into the car. I was the last to enter. A few stones were thrown by the remaining Arya Samaj, but no one was hurt.

After I left Nizamabad, a national minister named G.R. Purushotham continued the crusade. The meeting continued for many days.

One of my next stops was Marthanadam. I had almost refused to preach there, because Marthanadam is a city of only around twenty thousand people.

"Why should I hold a meeting in Marthanadam, with only twenty thousand people in the entire city, when—for the same expenditure of time and money—I can preach to a hundred thousand somewhere else?" I asked the nationals who invited me.

"Brother, we feel God would have you come to Marthanadam," they said. "Besides, you may get a larger audience than you think. Marthanadam is a bus center. People will be able to come to this crusade from all the surrounding cities."

After prayer, I decided to hold the crusade after all. I was glad I did. In that little town of twenty thousand, we had a turnout of well over a hundred thousand on the final night. The blind saw. The deaf heard. The dumb spoke.

The Marthanadam crusade sparked the most unusual Holy Spirit outpouring that I have ever witnessed. That whole city—in fact, that entire area—came to the Lord. It was a sovereign move of God. People were weeping and singing in the streets until two and three in the morning. The whole area seemed to be filled with the presence of God. I later heard that the revival continued for two and a half years after I left Marthanadam. And I had almost refused to go.

Not long after the Marthanadam crusade, I returned home to Houston to see my family and to raise the funds to hold yet another series of crusades. This time, I would need more funds than usual: it was summertime, the children were out of school, and Earnestine was eager to accompany me on another crusade. Her heart was in India, but during the school year, her duty lay at home.

We came to New Delhi during the Burning Loo. The Burning Loo is an oven-hot wind, a killer wind. During the night, it hit 110 degrees while we were there; daytimes, it reached 135 degrees. Following the nationals' advice, we were careful to stay out of the sun as much as possible. They didn't need to warn us twice: on the way to the hotel, we'd seen a man lying in the street, dead from sunstroke. A dog fed on his flesh.

We held the crusades on New Delhi's famous Ramlilla Grounds, the place where Mahatma Gandhi was assassinated. At first, the nationals working with us thought we would be unable to obtain permission to use the grounds. They were, after all, mainly used by the political superstars such as Indira Gandhi, Chou En Lai, and Eisenhower. And here was some comparatively unknown Texan preacher with the nerve to demand that they go and ask for the use of these grounds!

Some of my best preaching never gets heard by more than a handful. It seemed like I had to preach to those Indians for about an hour, but they finally got the message: they went and asked for the use of the grounds. They got it. Next, they started to worry about something else: if Mahatma Gandhi, who had been one of them, had been assassinated on Ramlilla Grounds, what would happen to Chris Panos, a foreigner and a Christian to boot? New Delhi is a stronghold of the Arya Samaj, and they were expected to cause trouble. One of the Indian pastors wrote me what he thought was an encouraging letter: "Come die for Christ!" he said.

Well, fortunately, I didn't die. In fact, during that particular crusade we had no trouble at all with political agitators. I had been believing God that we wouldn't: I had my wife and children with me, as well as Alliene and Wylie Vale, Houstonians who wanted to see a miracle crusade first hand.

The most dangerous part of the trip was the flight to Delhi from Bombay. We had caught only a few hours' sleep in Bombay, and I was napping on the plane. Suddenly, I awoke, aware that a battle was raging in the heavenlies as the devil sought to destroy our plane and its passengers. The plane was caught in a black dust storm. It was twisting and turning every which way, but we all joined in rebuking the tempestuous winds in the name of Jesus and landed safely.

As I went about the business of setting up the crusade, Earnestine and the children took in the sights: Hindu fakirs sitting on their beds of nails, snake charmers, the towers where the Parsis leave their dead. The Parsis are sunworshipers: they leave their dead on the tops of these towers for the vultures to eat. The Hindus, on the other hand, cremate their dead. Often, the New Delhi air was heavy with the sickly-sweet smell of burning bodies, their ashes blowing in the wind. And always, there were the people: the bearded, beturbaned Sikhs, fierce warriors from the North; the veiled Moslem women in their stifling ragged black wrappings; the pitiful masses of bone-thin poor dressed in threadbare rags. The unbelievers contrasted sharply with the clean and joyous Christian women in their gaily colored saris, and the stately elders clothed in white.

As usual, I preached a salvation sermon on the opening night.

Between eighty and ninety percent of the massive crowd prayed after me as I led them in the sinners' prayer. Then I prayed for God to confirm His word by healing the people of their diseases and infirmities, their bondages and deformities.

Immediately, little knots of movement broke out through the crowd as God touched the deaf, the crippled, the blind. A resounding crack sounded through the crowd as one woman, bent double for many years, began to straighten. As she started for the platform, becoming more and more erect, she raised her hands in praise to God. By the time she reached us, she was completely straight.

A child born clubfooted who had walked on the outside of his ankle was healed. When he stood upright on the sole and heel of his foot, you could see the rough, protruding callous on his ankle where he had dragged his foot along. He was ready to cry from shock.

"God healed you because He loves you," I said to him.

His face brightened immediately. "Jesus healed me!" he shouted.

Alliene Vale watched as a five-year-old girl's little club foot straightened in her husband's hand. Wylie Vale had been holding the little child whose other foot had been healed already. As he waited to tell the crowds about the healing, he examined the crippled foot. God chose just that moment to finish His healing work. It was a moving experience for her.

"One of my friends told me before we left that if I saw with my own eyes a real miracle, she would believe me," Alliene wrote home. "Now I can tell her that I did see with my own eyes miracles Jesus did when His word was preached in faith. The insane, the deaf, the blind, the cripples, and countless others were loosed and set free.

"Can you imagine our joy to see a five-year-old girl of Hindu parents (who were standing in the shadows), who had never stood or walked in her life, healed instantly? Words cannot express the floods of joy at His compassion in healing Muslims who left weeping and calling, 'Jesu, Jesu, we love you!' These were not 'vague improvements' that could be questioned by American rationalistic minds."

Chapter Thirty-One
The Charge of the Night Brigade!

I knew God had a purpose in our being on television, but it wasn't long before I was itching to get back to preaching the gospel live. I almost began to hate the television show, because it was keeping me here in America. I have nothing against preaching in America, but it does disturb me to spend all my time in a country where everybody has the opportunity to hear the gospel.

I felt hemmed in, tied down. I began to talk to God about it. Soon He showed me a way. In most of my crusades, the most time-consuming part is in setting it up. If I hired an advance man, I could teach him to do the setting up. I could then go overseas, losing only a minimal amount of time from television, and we could pre-record the programs for the days that I'd be gone.

As the advance man, I hired a slender soft-spoken car salesman named Glen Scott. Glen's father had been involved in a well-known healing ministry, but oddly—even though Glen had seen God perform many spectacular miracles—he

253

had not given his heart to the Lord as a child. But when he finally gave his heart to God, Glen was ready to give up a successful career and follow Jesus.

The first crusade Glen worked on was in Hubli, India. Back in the States, I'd gone over and over the things I wanted him to do in preparation for the crusade. He did them. But as soon as I arrived in Hubli, Glen asked to talk to me alone.

"India is nothing like I thought it would be," he said. "It's worse. Even the air here is syrupy with stench and oppression. I'm not sure if I'm cut out for this work. I've been wondering if I've missed my calling. I can't even feel the presence of God anymore. I *know* He will never leave me nor forsake me, but I *feel* like I left God back in the States."

"Almost everyone who comes here feels that way at first," I said. "Satan has had the people of India enslaved in heathen religions for so many years that you can just feel the oppression in the atmosphere. But we walk by faith, and not by feelings. Now is the time to stand on the word of God."

Glen decided to stay.

"I'm glad you decided to stick it out," I said. "I feel an unusual anointing. The Holy Spirit is just hovering, waiting to do something. I can't wait to find out what it is!"

The Catholic church had not as yet endorsed our meetings, but a number of Catholic nuns attended anyway. They had begun to hear reports of spiritual renewal from America. They wanted to see what was going on. We seated them on the platform along with the rest of the clergy.

That night, as I was preaching, I spoke of the unusual anointing that I felt.

As I spoke, a single white dove flew to the center of the clearing in front of the platform. When it lit, a little boy took off his braces and started running through the crowd. He broke into the clearing in front of the platform and headed straight for the dove. As he approached, it rose gracefully into the air. Later, Glen told me that it had flown straight to the center pole behind the platform, where it stayed till I finished my message.

The dove reappeared every evening for the rest of the crusade, perching on that center pole. Many healing miracles took place; in addition to that first little boy, a darling little girl named Vida also removed her braces and began to walk.

But it was the presence of the dove rather than the healing miracles which seemed to impress the Catholics most. Word spread like wildfire, and more and more nuns attended every evening. In fact, more and more people of every sort attended. Mysore State, in which Hubli is located, is not a very populous area, but by the last night of the crusade we had an attendance of one hundred thousand. The Hindus were enraged. Two groups joined forces towards the end of my sermon on the final night of the crusade and disrupted the power supply. The lights went out. We switched over to our emergency power supply, and they went back on again.

Meanwhile, I continued to preach. Towards the end of my sermon, I saw a commotion at the back of the field. A huge crowd of demonstrators (later estimated at thirty thousand) was trying to get to the speakers' platform. Inspired by God, I told the worshipers to be seated. The crowd sat. As the demonstrators slowly made their way to the platform, hampered now by the obstacle course provided by the masses of people sitting on the ground, I led the new converts in the sinners' prayer and prayed for the sick.

As the demonstrators approached, the national evangelists kept trying to get me to leave. Just as I finished praying, the demonstrators reached the platform area. By this time, everyone was in the car but me.

It was almost comical. I turned to go, and the demonstrators crowded forward. I stopped and looked around at them, and they froze in their tracks. I turned towards the car again, and they rushed forward. I stopped and looked around; they froze. I don't know why they froze whenever I looked at them, but I presume it was because—having seen so many miracles—they thought I might have some crowd-control miracles up my sleeve. If so, nobody wanted to be the first to experience one!

I reached the car ahead of the demonstrators and got in. Before we pulled away, I spoke to the chief of police, who was standing nearby. "I prophesy to you that the person who organized this demonstration will be stricken with a dread disease," I said. Later the man became paralyzed.

Quickly, we drove to the place where I'd been staying.

"Brother Panos, you must leave Hubli," said Philip Abraham, who had been helping with the crusade. "You have finished preaching here. Staying would be very dangerous. You must let us get you out of the city."

For some reason, I didn't mind.

"All right," I said. "Do what you think best." And so I left Hubli.

Chapter Thirty-Two
Terror Hits Two Hundred Thousand

After Hubli, we began to prepare for a crusade in Mangalore, which is also in Mysore State in India. Soon, Glen and I were both in Mangalore. We held the crusade on the Cricket Grounds. Once again, I'd had trouble getting the local pastors to request permission to hold a Christian meeting in the city's largest meeting place. The week before our crusade in Mangalore, Indira Gandhi spoke from those same grounds. Indira Gandhi always drew the biggest crowds in India; they couldn't understand why I would need facilities as big as the one that she used.

But we did get the permission that we needed. It was the first time a Christian meeting had been held on the Cricket Grounds.

Word of the Hubli miracles had run ahead of us to Mangalore. It seemed like the whole city had heard of us. Everywhere we went, people were talking about the leper who had been cleansed, and the cripples who had been healed.

Although we always have crowds of at least one hundred

thousand by the final night of a crusade, the first night crowds generally start small at around ten thousand. In Mangalore, the first-night crowd was fifty thousand. There were many pitiful cases. In my spirit, I sensed a special excitement, a feeling that God was going to move in a mighty way, not only on this first night, but throughout the whole crusade. Sure enough, He did. I preached that night on the Blood and the Cross.

As I preached, the power of God fell across the grounds and signs followed. So many people moved up front to give their testimony, that it looked like a stampede. And then there were the nuns. In India, Mangalore is known as the "Rome of the East" because of its many cathedrals and large Catholic population. Many nuns and priests had come to hear us speak that night. As the miracles progressed, the front of the platform seemed to blossom as the nuns in their white habits rose and lifted their arms in praise.

The next morning, many of the nuns and priests attended the seminar for clergy, and shared their testimonies.

"I had pain in my stomach," one sister said, "and it was cured by Jesus."

"One of my boys, a student who has been dumb for six years, is now speaking," Father Philip Rajvi said. I rejoiced. Father Rajvi was from the Orthodox church, a special brother in the Lord.

Sister Scholastica, mother superior of St. Anne's Convent, spoke to the gathering: "Most of the sisters feel we have increased our spiritual prayer and faith."

By the second night of the crusade, the crowds had swelled to one hundred thousand. That night, a beggar with long sticky, lice-filled hair was brought to the platform. He had been crippled for over six years, but Jesus had saved and healed him instantly.

"My name is Parameshwaran Nair," he said to the crowd.

"Six years ago, I had fever. From that time onwards I could not walk at all. I had to drag myself with my hands.

"Tonight I had an inner feeling as though someone was asking me to get up. I asked the two men who brought me to lift me up, and I began to walk."

From the rear of the platform, an Orthodox priest shouted, "I know this man! I know this man!"

I took a second look. It was Father Philip Rajvi, whose deaf and dumb student had been healed. "This man could not walk, and he begged for money at the bus station," Father Rajvi told us. "I know him well, for I have given him money every month for over five years."

On the third night of the crusade, the beggar was back on the platform to tell about his healing the night before. I didn't recognize him. Gone were the beard and the long, lice-filled hair. Gone was the burlap bag. Shaved, shorn, bathed, and dressed in a clean white suit that someone had given to him, he testified to the saving and healing power of Jesus Christ. Today, Parameshwaran Nair is ministering the gospel message in Bangalore.

Also on the third night, a girl named Celine Pinto was healed. Celine had been bedridden for nineteen years. This time the Catholic nuns shouted, "We know her! We know her!" Celine had spent most of her life in a Catholic hospital. One of the nuns was healed herself that same night. She had been scheduled for major surgery, but when she arrived at the Catholic hospital in Bangalore after the crusade was over, she told the Mother Superior General and her doctors that she had no further need for surgery. Many tests later, she was pronounced completely well.

The fourth night, the crowd was a record-breaking two hundred thousand. I just knew something exciting was going to happen. The previous evening, a brother's wife had had a vision.

"In my vision," she said, "I saw lights, like fireworks, all over the grounds. Showers of sparks would shoot up into the air, like Roman candles. It was just beautiful."

Vision or no vision, the fourth night began with difficulty. In order to harass us, Hindu agitators had set up a burlesque tent on the edge of the field. As I preached, snatches of honky-tonk music drifted across the grounds. But in spite of everything, God's presence settled sweetly upon the meeting. People were being saved and healed. The nuns were rejoicing and praising God.

Then it happened. Hindu saboteurs threw bicycle chains around the field's power lines. Sparks sprayed high into the air. The lights went out all over that whole section of the city. Here and there, people screamed as bits of molten metal from the sputtering power lines flew into the edge of the crowd.

Suddenly, I remembered that sister's vision: showers of sparks. God had known that this was going to happen, and He had allowed it. I knew then that He had everything in control.

As soon as our sound system was hooked up with the emergency battery, I resumed my sermon. God continued to move. In spite of all the devil had tried to do, we had more miracles than we could count.

On the fifth night, I introduced a national as the speaker.

"The miracles you have seen in this crusade are not the work of a man," I said to the crowd. "Even though I am not going to preach tonight, there will still be miracles. These miracles are not the work of a man, they are the work of God."

I moved to the back of the platform as the national began his sermon. A powerful anointing came over him as he began to speak. Miracles began to happen all over the grounds.

Midway through the sermon, Hindu agitators began to stone the platform. Other demonstrators threw huge double handfuls of sand at our faces, trying to get it in our eyes.

Many of the men on the platform were quite fearful, but the Catholic sisters stood like soldiers, praising God for the privilege of being persecuted for the sake of Christ. Here and there, a nun cried out in pain as sand got in her eyes, or a stone glanced off her body. One nun had her glasses knocked off. Blood streamed down her face, but she stood like another Joan of Arc. Miraculously, she wasn't seriously injured. Glen Scott was hit in the stomach by another stone, but its trajectory was almost spent by the time it reached him. He doubled over as the wind was knocked out of him.

God was with us. There were no deaths. Only one man needed medical care. He had been hit in the leg, but was not badly injured. None of those wonderful nuns needed to be taken to the hospital.

Throughout the whole disturbance, the national had continued to preach as though nothing unusual were happening. He was not hit by any of the stones. As he spoke, God confirmed His word with many miracles.

Glen and I left the grounds in separate cars. I was staying at the government house while Glen was staying in a hotel. Soon after I entered my room the phone rang. It was Glen.

"Chris," he said, "they're out to get me. As we drove to the hotel, we passed an enormous demonstration. The whole wide street was jammed with marching people—there must have been thousands of them—all yelling and waving signs."

"What did the signs say?"

"Get Glen Scott," he said succinctly.

"Why you?"

"Well, probably they're scared to go after you, after what happened to that man in Hubli. Evidently, they're not afraid of me."

"Well," I said, "they didn't get you yet."

"No, but they haven't quit trying. One of our workers just rushed up here to tell me to lock my window and bar my door. They're headed for this hotel, he says."

"Well," I laughed, "if they get you, Glen, I'll tell your wife you died a hero." In my spirit, I knew there was no danger. "Don't worry. Don't forget that you're surrounded by hosts of angels. You'll be okay."

And he was. Several miles separated the point where the demonstration had started from Glen's hotel. Long before the marchers had arrived where he was staying, the footsore rioters had disbanded and the demonstration had fizzled out.

It was another victory for God.

Chapter Thirty-Three
Straight From Jail

The next crusade was in Bangalore, the resort city of India, and no wonder. It must be the flower capital of the world. Even the trees were in flower. One tree that was in bloom while I was there was just one solid mass of blood-red flowers. Another tree was a mass of lavender. It was gorgeous.

By the time we hit Bangalore, we had the full support of the Catholic church. Archbishop Arokiaswamy met us at the airport, along with the mayor of Bangalore. Even Raj Bhavan, the governor of Mysore State, gave us his support.

Lutheran pastor Harald Bredesen joined us for the Bangalore crusade. He came straight from jail. Absent-mindedly, he'd left his passport in his other suitcoat and the authorities in New Delhi had locked him up while they sorted matters out.

On the first night of the crusade, a demon-possessed girl broke past the rope which kept the crowds away from the platform area. She was shouting and screaming. The workers tried to hold her, but I told them to let her go. Instantly, she headed in my direction.

"In the name of Jesus, fall down!" I ordered. To the great relief of the crowd, she did.

She lay flat on the ground until I finished preaching. Then I asked the ushers to bring her to the platform. Without any further ado, she came to the microphone and smiled joyfully as she accepted Jesus. She told the crowd that she was no longer tormented in any way.

Another night in Bangalore, a young man came running towards the platform shouting. He writhed on the ground like a snake, making ugly faces and weird noises.

"Be still!" I commanded. Immediately, he appeared to pass out. He lay there peacefully until the end of the meeting, when I had him brought to the platform.

"I accept Jesus," he cried out immediately. "I take Him as my Savior!"

"How do you feel?" I asked him.

"I feel wonderful. I am now completely free."

"How long had you been in that condition?"

"Twenty-one years."

In addition to Harald Bredesen, many other Christian businessmen attended the Bangalore crusade. "What really seemed to me as most outstanding," one wrote me later, "was the way the demons left those people."

Different things appealed to different people. O.M. Matthews, the Deputy Comptroller in Governor Raj Bhavan's office, seemed most impressed by healings.

"I was able to witness a number of sick people suffering from paralysis, cancer, epilepsy, etc., being healed and their coming to the dais and testifying their experience over the mike," he wrote me.

Harald Bredesen was happy about the miracles, but he

seemed most impressed by the outpouring of God's Spirit upon the Catholic nuns and priests.

"I have fallen in love," Harald told Pat Robertson on the *700 Club*. "I've fallen in love with 200 Catholic nuns!"

Harald was a great blessing as he ministered to the Catholic nuns and priests in the morning clergy meetings.

"You know, I didn't think that Chris was called to preach," Harald told Pat Robertson. "When he went to preach the gospel, I thought he was meant to be a businessman, not a preacher. But after the Bangalore crusade, I know that I was wrong."

Like Harald, I, too had fallen in love with the many lovely Catholics of Mysore State. Perhaps that is why I was so very touched when I received a letter from Archbishop Arokias-wamy.

"Dear Brother Chris Panos," he wrote, "I am extremely happy about the Miracle Life Crusade you conducted here in Bangalore . . . Every one could sense that you are fully committed to Christ and that, like St. Paul, you are eager to preach Christ and Him Crucified."

St. Paul is one of my favorite Bible characters. I was deeply moved by being compared to him. Especially by an archbishop!

"I am glad you made it plain right from the beginning," the archbishop continued, "that you do not claim to be a miracle worker, and that God alone has the power to work miracles . . . God bless you and your apostolate of preaching Christ."

It was a beautiful end for a spectacular crusade.

Chapter Thirty-Four
The Last Challenge

Of all the crusades that I have held in India, the one in Nagpur stands out most vividly in my mind. Perhaps the reason Nagpur still seems so vivid is because it was the last I held before this book was finished.

Enormous crowds and innumerable miracles made the Nagpur crusade an overwhelming success. The mayor of Nagpur, B.M. Gaikwad, came out to meet me at the airport, enormous crowds massed to hear the gospel, and even the Indian newsmen gave the Nagpur crusade outstanding coverage. This was a miracle in itself, since their Hindu-owned newspapers are usually quite hostile to the gospel.

The Nagpur crusade started on a Thursday. Early, early in the morning, the crowds began to gather at the Kastur-chand Park Ground, waiting patiently in the hot Indian sun for the time when the evening crusade would start. An Indian film-maker volunteered to make a movie of the crusade.

Early in the crusade, I taught the people to praise the

Lord. The crowd stood, and following our instructions, they raised their hands. The field was about six hundred yards long, and about three hundred and fifty yards wide. As the people stood waving their outstretched hands in praise, they reminded me of a gigantic wheatfield. I understood what Jesus had meant when He talked of "fields white to harvest."

On the first night of the crusade, a Malayan lady, the wife of a driver in the fire brigade, brought two of her four children to the platform. Her two sons had been born deaf and dumb. Her husband had given up all hope of his sons' ever being able to talk, but when we tested the ten-year-old, young Jay Prakash, he admitted he could hear. His astounded mother burst into tears. Her other son was healed as well.

Another ear healing that night was a Sikh lady, the wife of a building contractor, who had not been able to hear from her left ear for the past three years.

"I tried practically every hospital, both in Nagpur and in Delhi," she testified. "I was undergoing treatment, but nothing had helped. When I heard of this meeting, I came hoping for a miracle. Now I have hearing in both ears."

Other ear healings included a forty-five-year-old tailor from the Sadar area who had been deaf in one ear, and a medical doctor in the government hospital in Chandrapur. He had tried every treatment that he knew without success, but within minutes of arriving at the meeting, he could hear clearly with both ears. He was so moved he could hardly express his joy.

In addition to the many ear healings in Nagpur, there were other miracles of all descriptions. Growths and tumors disappeared, cripples walked, and the demon-possessed were freed and saved. And as always, multitudes accepted Jesus Christ, which is the greatest miracle of all.

The Nagpur crusade started on a Thursday. Crowds built

quickly on Friday and Saturday. "And the next sabbath day" (to quote Acts 13:44) "came almost the whole city together to hear the word of God." Attendance was estimated at over one hundred thousand on Sunday alone, and many thousands were saved and healed. Again, there were too many miracles for us to count. But no matter how many miracles I had in Nagpur, no matter how many miracles I have in any city, it will not be enough. That is why I wrote this book: to challenge you, the reader, to go into all the world and preach the gospel.

The gospel witness that Jesus Christ is the Son of God is the most important news of any day. When it first was heard, it spread like wildfire as the presence of God's Holy Spirit—indwelling fishermen, farmers, tent makers, and civil servants—turned men with hearts of flesh into flaming, burning evangelists who pointed the masses toward the only source of salvation: Jesus Christ, the Son of the Living God.

This same power is available to you. With God's power, you too can reach all the nations of the world. There are no closed doors to the gospel. And God wants you to go.

As I write this, the field lies white to harvest, like the harvest field in Nagpur. The world lies dying, poisoned by sin. The antidote is Jesus. You may not be called the way I was to tell His story. You do not need some kind of special vision. God is already waiting for you to meet the challenge. And He has already issued you your marching orders: "Go ye into all the world, and preach the gospel to every creature" (Mark 16:15).

Go ye.

For a complimentary copy of *Far East Reporter* or for
additional information and speaking engagements:

Chris Panos
P.O. Box 3333
Houston, TX 77253

Phone: 1-800-97-FRESCO
E-mail: chrispanos@pdq.net
Web pages: http://freeweb.pdq.net/chrispanos